Mate in 7

Master of own destiny

José C. Rodrigues

Jul, 2023

I want to thank Syed Hasan Mehdi, author of the image used on the cover of this book and freely disclosed at "pexels.com."

Index

This page was intentionally left blank.

Preamble

I learned to play chess from my father. He taught me the basic rules of moving pieces when I was still a child. During my childhood and adolescence, we played chess from time to time, at the weekend or after dinner, always in a fun and relaxed way.

I entered the University of Economics in 1989. I was being seen at the front door when, while they were painting my face with lipsticks in the Faculty colors, green and white, another freshman asked me: "So, where are you coming from?" It was there that I met Ricardo, who came from Elvas. Later, I met Manuel. A freshman with a thick beard, always two or more days long, very dark skin tone, and a bit lacking in hair. He looked like a person with a criminal file. We all became friends for life.

Ricardo was an amateur chess player. He had participated in tournaments, had trained regularly at the local chess club, had studied the basic opening, middle, and endgame techniques, and had an arsenal of pitfalls typical of someone who takes chess at least seriously. Inevitably, he took his chessboard to Lisbon.

One day, during the first semester, I went to meet Ricardo and Manuel at the "Colégio Universitário Pio XII," where Ricardo had a rented room. We had time and Ricardo proposed an unusual game of chess. He prepared to play against me, with his back to the board, without seeing the pieces. The rules were as follows. Ricardo was playing white and we both had to give quick answers, in a few seconds, indicating the coordinates of the move; such as: "rook f8 c8". Manuel kept an eye on the game to ensure that there were no mistakes in moving the pieces. I accepted the challenge. And so we began a unique and interesting experience.

We both started the game in automatic mode. Ricardo played his favorite opening by heart. With his back to the board, and with his eyes closed so that nothing would interfere with his memorization of the position of the pieces, he would give the coordinates of his moves in seconds, as agreed. I, devoid of the most elementary basic notions of the game, responded instinctively. At a certain point, Ricardo gives an instruction to move a knight, like "knight f6 d5". I had Black at a clear disadvantage on the board and felt like I needed more time to think. So, I retorted: "Oh man, Ricardo!... You don't have any knights on f6"... I lied! And right after, Manuel bursts out laughing.

We had many good times together, but I hold this one in my heart with special gratitude. The way I lost the chess game, to an opponent who had his back to the board, was due to countless factors, but more important than my lack of preparation to face an opponent who was far superior, was my total ignorance of the most elementary strategies inherent to the game of chess. Since then, I began to value the knowledge and abilities of any person. I started to give even more importance to deepening my knowledge of any and all subjects that interested me.

In 1993, I finished the Economics course. I managed to finish in four years a course that was supposed to take five. I took more subjects per semester than was normally recommended, accumulating the necessary credits to obtain the Bachelor of Economics degree from Universidade Nova de Lisboa, which is now known as Nova School of Business and Economics. I was told that I was an economist. I had some economics knowledge. I had some math skills. I had some notions of statistics. I had some accounting skills. I had a notion of law. I had some management skills. I had some notions of how to speak English. I did not know how to do anything really...

I went to work for a bank. I learned the rules of work of the institution. They did not explain it to me, but I always tried to understand why such a rule was created and why such a procedure was adopted. I was six years at the bank. I came to the conclusion that the multiplicity of rules and procedures did not always suit the concrete situations posed by real life. Often, instead of simplifying the lives of employees and customers, rules and procedures were used in a perverse way, resulting in a consequence contrary to what was intended at the time of their creation. At other times, the rules were not evenly applied. Finally, rules, procedures, and people were often simply, and insolently, disregarded. After a certain point, I could not stand it anymore. I got out.

Since then, I have worked for several employers, been a partner in companies, completed a master's degree in international business, and never stopped studying economics. I have always understood that, out of respect for my academic training as an economist, it is my duty to be able to explain to anyone how society improves their levels of well-being. And I must do so logically and free of any bias or opinion.

I understood that the cause-and-consequence relationships that are established in the functioning of society go deeper than what human intuition allows to be achieved. At the moment, destructive protests are taking place in Paris, the entire civil service is on strike in Portugal, Ukrainian cities are bombed by the Russian army, two banks in the United States have just failed, Credit Suisse has just been saved by the central bank of his country, and hundreds of similar events take place around the world, with a special focus on South America. The construction of a free society, without inflation, without unemployment, without economic crises, and in which people freely adopt positive behaviors is relatively simple. But the construction of this almost poetic reality requires an understanding of the strategies that human beings use to condition their own behavior. And this is the background theme that is herein analyzed.

I am hoping that society will not repeat my mistake and allow the opponent to win the game with his back to the board.

This page was intentionally left blank.

Bounded rationality

Garry Kasparov and Anatoly Karpov are two of the greatest chess masters ever. They dominated world chess in the last two decades of the 20th century. Between the two, they played 144 games, with 104 draws, 21 wins for Kasparov, and 19 wins for Karpov. The deep knowledge that both had of the game led to such a significant balance in the results obtained in the matches against each other.

The development of a good chess player takes place through constant evolution and is divided between individual study and the game against the most diverse opponents. The clash with different opponents widens the range of situations with which the chess player learns to deal with. The individual study allows one to deepen the reasoning regarding the consequences that are obtained through the successive moves with which one tries to reach the final position of advantage on the board.

One of the individual exercises that allow the chess player to improve his calculation capacity in the game is the "mate in 3." In practice, the student is confronted with a wide range of different situations for the distribution of pieces on the board, in which it is possible to checkmate the opponent with only three moves on his part. Given that each chess player alternates the execution of each move, one of the most interesting components of this exercise is the fact that we know, unequivocally, that our three moves will result in our victory, according to the rules of the game, and whatever the two moves the opponent chooses to make in response to our own. Knowing the rules of the game is not enough to be an expert in the field. The ability to deepen our understanding of a chain of cause-and-effect relationships determines the level of rationality that human beings can achieve in a given domain.

In 1996, with the increasing development of so-called supercomputers, IBM created a chess-playing machine called Deep Blue, consisting of 256 co-processors and which was allegedly capable of analyzing 200 million positions per second. The company challenged Garry Kasparov to a game between man and machine. The man won three games, drew two, and lost one. The six-game clash was repeated again in 1997, this time with Kasparov recording two defeats, three draws, and just one win. The results gave rise to a long history of controversies and subsequent developments related to the greater or lesser capacity of artificial intelligence in relation to humans.

From then on, humanity began to confuse the concepts of "intelligent use of software" with "use of intelligent software."

The way Deep Blue defeated Garry Kasparov has come under close scrutiny. Until 1996, the development of Deep Blue was based on the sharing of knowledge carried out by humanity regarding the best practices in the game of chess. The computer's memory was filled up with a database made of more than 700,000 games of Masters and Grand Masters. Then, between the clashes of 1996 and 1997, it was recognized that the computer was severely intervened by programmers in an improvement process. Finally, there were incidents that induce rational thinking. Some of these curiosities are the following: 1) IBM publicly acknowledged that it made adjustments to the program between each game played, a situation that demonstrates Deep Blue's difficulty in learning by itself; 2) IBM refused to provide Kasparov with the reports of some chess games played by Deep Blue, a situation that gave Kasparov the disadvantage of not being able to try to understand his opponent under the same circumstances that the computer could understand him; and 3) when Kasparov asked for a third tournament to be held, IBM, without we can truly understand why, simply refused. Deep Blue is an example of the use of human capacity in the search for the best use of available information.

In the chess realm, it is known that Garry Kasparov had a calculation depth of up to fifteen moves. He is one of the best human beings ever to master the game of chess. But, far beyond the natural talent that he necessarily possesses for the game of chess, the development of this capacity was due to the accumulated experience of his individual study combined with the clashes with other great human beings endowed with the same potential; as was the case with Anatoly Karpov. Both specialized in the game of chess.

A chess game often begins with the move "pawn e2 e4." From the outset, this move makes it possible to put into practice the most basic strategic principles to win the game, such as dominating the central squares and making room for the development of the greatest possible number of white pieces on the board. However, Masters, and Grand Masters, often start their game with a different move. In order to choose a certain course of action, much more important than following the most elementary rules and principles, commonly defined, it is crucial to understand why.

Psychology explains that emotional thinking always precedes the development of logical reasoning. The human decision-making mechanism is often based on intuition. Neurologists, such as António Damásio, and psychologists, such as Daniel Kahneman, claim that, under the right circumstances, intuitive thinking comes to mind spontaneously, without effort, causing the human reaction to having an emotional basis before it can be properly thought through. Psychologists deepen this line of reasoning even further by proving that only the mental installation of a doubt process can stimulate logical reasoning. Human beings find it difficult to deal simultaneously with seemingly incompatible concepts regarding a given subject. It is through individual doubt, about what might be the best decision to make, that reasoning ability is consolidated.

It is known today that the brain is one of the organs of the body that consumes the most energy. Consequently, emotional decision-making allows human beings to save energy. Deciding based on previously acquired beliefs and prejudices is a process that facilitates decision-making. Psychologists have found that the mind's accessibility to statistical information is slow. But this process can be improved through training and resorting to the use of relevant rules for the objective to be achieved. Although this is a tiring process, so that rational thinking can reach more advanced levels, it is necessary to remove the emotional "certainties" that our brain anticipates and replace them with doubts about the best path to follow.

When doubt is not consciously considered, human beings show the most primitive behaviors and make the least correct decisions to guarantee their own well-being. Thus, precipitated decision-making arises, which is, in these cases, always based on institutional processes.

The way in which institutions work, simultaneously, as a process that facilitates decision-making and inhibits rational thinking, can be seen through the use of the experimental method. At this level, scientists carried out an experiment with chimpanzees to understand how it is possible to condition individual decision-making after establishing a certain culture of collective action.

Four chimpanzees were placed in a large cage. The animals could roam freely on the floor of the cage. This was spacious enough for the four monkeys and had a significant height. On one of the walls, a few meters high, there was a small window that allowed the scientists access to the interior of the cage. The scientists placed a narrow ladder, where only one monkey could climb at a time. On the ground, the animals were fed with trivial feed. After a period in which the caged animals had adapted to their reality, the scientists introduced a disturbance factor which consisted of opening the high window and placing a splendid and appetizing bunch of bananas at the top of the stairs. Immediately, the monkey closest to the base of the stairs began to climb and enjoyed the magnificent delicacy. This procedure was repeated and the monkeys began to position themselves closer and closer to the ladder, each with the expectation to be the only one to reach the bunch of bananas when it appeared.

Then, a second perturbation factor is introduced by the scientists. From that moment on, whenever the desired bunch of bananas was placed at the top of the stairs, after a monkey had climbed up and while it was feasting on the fruits, the scientists began to wet the three animals that were on the ground with cold water. The cold water shower was only applied after the arrival of a monkey to the bananas.

The animals' reaction did not delay. After a period of

adaptation to the situation, whenever a bunch of bananas was placed at the top of the stairs and a chimpanzee started to climb, the remaining monkeys on the ground threw themselves at him, holding him, attacking him, and preventing his arrival to the bunch of bananas. Until a monkey hit the bananas, the scientists did not wet any monkeys in the soil.

After a short time, after all the animals realized that the reaction of those on the ground would be to hit the individual who tried to reach the bananas, the chimpanzees stopped climbing the ladder to reach the bananas. And these could rot at the top of the stairs...

From then on, the scientists removed one of the chimpanzees from the cage and placed a new animal inside. At the first appearance of the bananas, the new animal ran to the stairs, started to climb, and the remaining three animals, seniors in the cage, threw themselves at it, grabbed it, prevented the continuation of the climb, and attacked it. The procedure was repeated until the new animal stopped trying to reach the bananas.

At this point, the cage had three animals from the initial group, which had been wet with the cold water shower, and one animal that had never been wet before.

Then, the scientists removed one more animal from the initial group of the cage and introduced a new chimpanzee. Once again, faced with the appearance of the bunch of bananas, the most recent animal in the cage tried to climb the ladder and reach the bananas, but was stopped by the remaining three members of the group. No animals have been wet as no monkeys got to the bananas. The scientists repeated the experiment, removing, one by one, the two animals that remained from the initial group, having always encountered an immediate reaction of aggression on the part of the monkeys on the ground when the new chimpanzee tried to climb the ladder to reach the bananas. The scientists then arrived at a situation in which, on the ground, there were four animals that had never been wet, but that persisted in attacking the others whenever they tried to reach the bunch of bananas.

We cannot talk to the chimpanzees. However, if we asked each of the four initial monkeys why they attacked the others and prevented them from reaching the bananas, they would answer that they did not like to be wet with a cold shower. Now, if we could ask each of the last four monkeys that inhabited the cage why they wanted to attack the chimpanzee that climbed the ladder to reach the bananas, they could only answer something like "I do not know, but it has always been done this way…"

Stimulating the development of critical thinking cannot be achieved without a good communication base. To improve the welfare levels of the group, the last chimpanzee to enter the cage would need to be able to communicate with the others. But, the fact of putting the rules in doubt, the fact of questioning the institutional environment that we do not always understand, does not mean that our well-being is called into question. Quite often, the exact opposite happens. We compromise our quality of life due to the perpetuation of the lack of communication.

A mundane and illuminating example comes out from the trivial articulation between a military institution and a city official. In a certain city, there was a military barracks whose entrance was permanently guarded by a soldier. Outside the barracks, the city had a public garden with a garden bench near the entrance to the military facility. One day, a city official was assigned to renew the painting of the garden benches and also painted the bench that was close to the entrance to the barracks. The civil servant went to the guard on duty and asked him to call the officer on duty. When the officer on duty arrived, he was told that the bench had been freshly painted and that no one could sit there. The officer on duty told the guard that no one could sit on that bench in the garden and that he had to pass the word on to the soldier who was coming next to relieve him. From that moment on, and for a long time, the guard on duty prevented anyone from sitting on the garden's bench. Until someone asked why...

Human behavior is essentially irrational because we consciously choose to refuse to think. Just like the ill-prepared chess player, we enter behavioral lines based on poorly understood institutional principles and act in a certain way without questioning why. We proceed in "monkey mode." We do things in a certain way simply because it has always been done like that. And, if this has always been done this way, we can hardly be criticized. Based on prejudice, we do things convinced of our emotional certainties.

Humanity's most recent history has provided us with numerous examples of our bounded rational capacity. One of the most notable, not only for the media coverage it acquired but above all for the way it highlights the effect of prejudice on decision-making, is known as the "Monty

Hall Problem."

Monty Hall was the stage name of Maurice Halperin, an individual who hosted a television contest in the United States. The contest ran from 1963 until 1986. The host presented several games to the audience. Contestants had the opportunity to choose between keeping the prizes already won or exchanging them for unknown prizes, existing behind three doors. However, the Monty Hall problem became known in 1990 after the show went off the air. At the time, Marilyn vos Savant was a writer and columnist for the popular magazine "Parade" and had a space dedicated to her called "Ask Marilyn." In this space, readers asked questions about mathematics and advanced science, which were answered by her.

One day in September 1990, a reader posed a question that became known as the "Monty Hall Problem." The problem is quite interesting. Suppose you are in a television contest and you are given the chance to choose a prize that is behind each of the three doors that are closed in front of you. The presenter informs that behind two of the doors is a goat and that behind the other door is a magnificent automobile. Then the presenter asks you to choose a door. After the competitor has chosen a door, the presenter opens one of the two remaining ones, shows him a goat, and asks him if he wants to keep the prize, which is behind the door he chose, or if he prefers to change it. Is it advantageous for you to accept the exchange?

This seemingly simple problem induces most people to stick to their starting position. In the final moment, when he has to make the last decision, the competitor is looking at two doors and is perfectly aware that, behind one of them is the desired car, and behind the other is a goat. Apparently, the common human being is induced to think that he is facing a fifty-fifty situation and, in that case, he chooses to maintain his initial position. Some people even claim that we have to stay with our initial gut!

Marilyn vos Savant responded to her reader by informing that not only is it in her best interest to accept the trade, but by doing so, she doubles her chance of winning the car.

This response triggered unexpected reactions across the country, even from mathematicians and university professors, with thousands of letters being addressed to the magazine "Parade" protesting against the response given to the reader. Marilyn vos Savant reported that nine out of ten readers disagreed with her resolution of the problem. The pressure exerted on the magazine, and on the writer, was such that she felt obliged to publish a second article explaining the solution, on February 17, 1991. Despite her efforts, the dispute was only definitively eradicated when, on July 21, 1991, John Tierney published an article in the "New York Times" journal in defense of Marylin vos Savant.

Effectively, at first sight, and for any one of us, it seems that we are facing a fifty-fifty solution, but this wrong intuition happens because we mentally position ourselves in the evaluation of the final situation and disregard the route taken that led us to the moment of taking the last decision. At the beginning of the problem, the competitor can choose between two goat doors and one car door. Your chance of success in hitting the car with the first choice is 1 in 3 (or ⅓) and the chance of getting it wrong with the first choice is 2 in 3 (or ⅔). Thus, whenever the competitor accepts the exchange proposed by the presenter, at the final moment, he will reverse his initial situation, that is, he will win whenever he chose wrong the first time, and doubles his possibility of success!

When we combine our limitations to unbiased thinking with a fear-based emotional state, we make decisions that are not best for us. Regrettably, and similarly to what the mathematicians and university professors who decided to challenge Marilyn vos Savant's solution by addressing letters to the magazine "Parade" did, we begin by presenting a position of strength before trying to understand the reason for the difference in position presented by the other people. Unfortunately, we tend to act on intuition and thereby reduce our potential to succeed.

We, humans, are incredibly less capable animals than what we normally believe ourselves to be. Our reasoning capacity is very limited and the belief that we are rational animals must be questioned. Between provocation and conviction, there is an unfilled space of understanding.

But human beings learn how to think. As the chess player does, it is through the recognition of our abilities and limitations that progress occurs. We ask: "Why?" We run away from prejudices. We cast doubt on a particular line of reasoning. We raise possibilities of action-consequence. We identify the optimal solution. And we understand how we got there. From then on, we build on the knowledge gained.

This page was intentionally left blank.

Adversary

The great rivalry between Anatoly Karpov and Garry Kasparov is just one more among the many that we can identify whenever two contemporary human beings have high-level performances in the same area of expression. Sport is fertile in these situations. For example, in the last fifty years, we can identify the cases of Alain Prost – Ayrton Senna, Michael Jordan – Magic Johnson, Steffi Graf – Martina Navratilova, Mike Tyson – Evander Holyfield, and Cristiano Ronaldo – Leonel Messi. In a first analysis, more than the enemy to be shot down, the opponent is an entity from whom we can learn. And mutual admiration and respect can be cemented.

In this context, the possibilities of learning through competition are cemented when players commit themselves to the pursuit of victory without resorting to dishonest expedients. If not, the winner will attribute his success to the use of resources that have nothing to do with the competition and, naturally and consciously, devalues even his own performance.

But emotional reactions precede rational thinking. If the needs for recognition and immediate success take precedence over a higher desire for long-term consistency, then the individual naturally tends to carry out any type of practice that leads to victory, regardless of the future effects that this action may have. In 2003, Daniel Kahneman, and his peers, warned that human beings favor the pursuit of certain results, instead of uncertain ones, and that the long-term vision can be sterile, insofar as the long term is not where life happens. Faced with this alert from Psychology, we realize that dishonest behavior toward opponents, more than a reality, can be a constant.

Economics explains that people seek to take advantage of the circumstances the environment provides them. By seizing an opportunity to improve their living conditions, each individual can trigger different consequences for themselves and others. The opportunistic behavior developed by a person, in order to improve their well-being, can be classified as negative or positive. Negative opportunistic behavior occurs when someone acts to satisfy their own needs, although they are aware that they will end up worse off if everyone else in the community acts in the same way. Examples of negative opportunistic behavior are stealing or bribing. On the other hand, positive opportunistic behavior happens when the person acts to satisfy his own needs, fully aware that he himself will be even better off if the whole community behaves in the same way. Examples of positive opportunistic behavior are the production of goods and services or acts to avoid polluting the planet. It is in the type of opportunistic behavior that we adopt that lies the essence of the stages of development, or decay, of a society.

Mankind's recent history is full of situations in which opportunistic behavior manifests itself intensely in each of the two ways. However, and in a very enlightening way as to the relevance that opportunistic behavior has in the stage of progress, or decline, in the living conditions of populations, the history of humanity provides us with very striking examples through two slightly more remote events.

In ancient Greece, approximately six hundred years before Christ, the Greek territory was distributed over several regions, which were even more fragmented between cities, islands, and small territories. Each territory had a lord, who ruled unopposed and entirely according to his will. It was the aristocrat – a term that results from the combination of aristos, which means "better", with kratein, which means "to rule". Each aristocrat subjugated the populations of his territory as he pleased. The aristocrat was chosen by the population mainly because he was the richest. He was the one who could provide weapons in case of need for defense against potential invaders. He was the one who could afford to pay for the entertainment of the community by hiring musicians and dancers. And he was also the one who decided conflicts between the citizens of his territory. However, in addition to popular choice, power was also gained through war.

In 546 B.C., a man emerged in Athens who gained power by force. He was called Pisistratus and ruled in a completely different way than the aristocrats of the time. He began by developing the notion of the nation-state in the population. He encouraged the lower classes of the population to recognize allegiance to the state and not to any aristocrat, whatever his wealth. He encouraged the participation of the common people in public affairs. He centralized public administration. He emptied of meaning the functions of the aristocracy within the society. He imposed a ten percent tax on all land and used that money to subsidize poorer farmers. He stimulated the development of the ceramics industry and commercial exchanges with the outside of Athens, extending them throughout the Aegean Sea. He built several public infrastructures to support the private sector. He encouraged festivals and the arts. He established a fruitful relationship between all people in society. Pisistratus showed how economic and social development can be achieved when the community is encouraged to adopt positive opportunistic behaviors. He ruled Athens from 546 B.C. to 527 B.C..

However, at the time, humanity was not able to understand that the essence of joy and prosperity lies in the community's ability to continually provide itself with the stimuli for positive opportunistic behavior. Since then, we have mostly adopted negative opportunistic behaviors, and, a thousand years later, we were still living in medieval times.

In particular, in the twelfth century, in Mongolia, similar to what had happened in Athens more than a thousand years before, the Mongol territories were also divided into several tribes, each ruled by a lord, the "khan." The Mongols accepted that power over the tribe was passed from father to son. But, this rule was often ignored and power was simply gained by force. Relations with the other tribes were a mixture of alliances and betrayals. The resort to weapons, and the art of war, was constant.

It is supposed that, in 1162, Temudjin was born, the son of Yesugei, then leader of a Mongol tribe. At the age of thirteen, Temudjin, along with his father, went to the territory of a neighboring tribe to choose a wife and restore peace between the clans. But his father was poisoned on the way back.

Taking advantage of the death of Temudjin's father, a former soldier of Yesugei, named Targutai, expelled Temudjin's entire family from the tribe's territory and forced them to survive in the steppes with meager means. Temudjin had a cousin named Jamukha, with whom he shared many of the hardships of that time, and there are records that they even shared the last food reserves. It is said that, during his youth, Temudjin was forced into constant escape as Targutai's pursuit was persistent. As a result of this experience, Temudjin became an expert in archery shooting and was able to ride all day long. Throughout this period, Temudjin never failed to establish contact with those who might become his allies. At the age of seventeen, he married Borte, who was from a neighboring tribe, his father's former ally, the Onggirat. Little by little, his father's old men allied with Temudjin over Targutai, and before he was twenty he was made head of the tribe.

He was always committed to uniting all the "khan" in a single force commanded by him. Relentless in the pursuit of his objective, he was extremely generous with the chiefs who served under his orders, but he did not admit a rival and killed anyone who could share, or dispute, power with him. He followed a nomadic path through the lands of Mongolia, preaching the unification of clans. With him followed his cousin Jamukha. However, the latter never accepted being Temudjin's subordinate and ended up moving away. This separation resulted in the splitting of the entire Mongolia in two, with many clans associated with Temudjin, and many others associated with Jamukha. In 1201, the two forces faced each other, in what became known as "The Battle of the Thirteen Sides." And Temudjin won. Unfazed, he ordered Jamukha's death. Five years later, in 1206, he was proclaimed "Genghis Khan," the clan of clans.

From then on, he conceived the concept of "total war" and organized his followers in support of his goals.

Nothing was left to chance, and both the preparation of his forces for war and the detailed study of the enemy were developed with great depth. The army was divided in a vertical command structure into contingents of ten units: ten, one hundred, one thousand, or ten thousand men. Each unit of greatness had a commander. In this way, "Genghis Khan" effectively commanded an army of two hundred thousand men dealing directly with his generals. The army had auxiliary troops to handle catapults, arsenal handlers, and even a section for lost objects. The attention to weaponry was taken to the point of exhaustion. He instituted the curved bow for use with the horse in motion and combined its use with the longbow. He created three different types of arrows to be used depending on the conditions of battle. The arrows, for close-range combat, were heavy and had a steel tip to penetrate the enemy's protective breastplates. His army was trained intensely and at the same time studied the enemy in detail. Before attacking, he used to previously introduce trusted people into the territories he planned to conquer. He used to look for disaffected people among the enemy people to take advantage of these hostilities against the local power. He was previously advertising his barbarities in the enemy territories he was preparing to conquer. He had always annihilated the conquered peoples, killing men, women, and children. Between 1207 and 1227, he conquered a territory that reached 24 million square kilometers, encompassing the territories of Mongolia, China, the Middle East, and part of the territories of southern Russia and Ukraine.

A deeper analysis of these two realities allows for drawing interesting conclusions regarding humanity's greatest adversary. On the one hand, Pisistratus's society based its line of action on the inclusion and involvement of all members of the population in a behavioral process that allowed the entire community to prosper. The activity developed by Pisistratus brought benefits to humanity, which, in addition to those verified for the Athenians themselves, also extended to all the peoples with whom Athens established commercial exchanges. In Athens, there was a clear notion that the population could improve their living conditions if their socio-economic organization was replicated by other cities or states because that would result in even more favorable exchange conditions. On the other hand, the society of Genghis Khan savagely committed itself to the conquest of an enormous empire, fully aware that its survival would be put into question if an opponent with the same, or superior, military cunning appeared. Temudjin always knew he was in danger if other people had the same kind of goals as he did. In both situations, the achievements reached were ephemeral. Both concentrated executive power in a single person. Humanity's only opponent is the absence of a collective awareness of how positive opportunistic behavior is consolidated. We are in competition with ourselves.

Value

The chess set consists of two sets of sixteen pieces, one white and the other black. White or black, each set has exactly the same number of pieces of equal value. The pieces are as follows: a king, a queen, two bishops, two knights, two rooks, and eight pawns. By convention, the first move belongs to the white pieces. The value of each piece depends on its power to perform a certain action, in conjunction with the position the piece occupies on the board.

The most valuable piece is the king. The objective of the game is to submit the opponent's king to the situation of checkmate. In this situation, the king is captured and the game is over. The king, the most valuable piece on the board, has the value of life.

Due to the movement powers that the rules attribute to each piece, and just so that the beginner in the game of chess has an idea of the relative importance that each piece has to help win the game, the following values are usually assigned to the remaining pieces: queen, 9; tower, 5; bishop, 3; horse, 3; and pawn, 1. It is also explained, early on, that the loss of a piece equal to, or greater than, 3 points is such a disadvantage that the player will only avoid losing the game if the opponent also commits in the future one or more errors of similar severity. However, it is also explained that a two-pawn disadvantage assumes the same degree of relevance. Finally, it should be noted that each pawn, in addition to the support it gives to the movement of other pieces of greater value, has, by itself, decisive importance when it manages to reach the opposite side of the board because, once reached the final line on the opponent's field, the pawn can be promoted to the Queen! It thus follows that the chess player cannot forget about any piece.

As in the game of chess, the conception of value varies, not only from person to person but also depending on the situation each individual faces. In 1776, Adam Smith explained that the word "value" has two different meanings: 1) it sometimes expresses the utility that a given object has, and 2) at other times it expresses the purchasing power that the possession of that object provides to its holder. We are thus faced with two different concepts of value: use value and exchange value. Economics deepens these concepts even further by emphasizing that the very notion of value varies according to circumstances, even considering the same individual. For example, a glass of water in summer can be much more valuable to us than the same glass of water in winter. However, both in the case of use value, in which we appreciate the satisfaction we get from drinking a glass of water and in the case of exchange value, in which we take the opportunity to sell the glass of water we own for a higher price, it is the ultimate goal of satisfying our needs that determines whether a good has value for us.

It is interesting to analyze the conception of value that was dominant in the societies of Pisistratus and Genghis Khan.

Pisistratus's society developed agricultural productivity and the pottery industry. It dedicated itself to the production of agricultural surpluses and artifacts in clay, fabrics, and other goods. He produced far beyond his needs and began trading with the people around him. By contacting other people, he was also providing them with the same type of improvement in well-being through the exchange of surpluses. Athenians and other peoples with whom they deprived, all had a much greater number of goods at their disposal than would have happened if they had self-limited to producing for themselves. And, in this regard, each good produced simultaneously acquired use value and exchange value. Exchange value is thus defined by the utility that the use of a good, which is superfluous for the producer, can mean for another consumer. And, in addition to providing a broad application of use value, Pisistratus also knew how to create and develop exchange value.

Genghis Khan, for his part, chose the territories to conquer based on the size of the herds that existed there, the potential for weapons that could be appropriated, and the fertility of the soil to guarantee good pastures. It is not known that he ever embarked on commercial efforts to carry out exchanges of goods with anyone. Only use-value had meaning to him. Due to a lack of knowledge, Mongolian society missed the opportunity to improve its living conditions by resorting to exchange mechanisms.

Psychology provides us with an important clue that could explain the reasons why, over the centuries, humanity has still not been able to concentrate on the generalized consolidation of positive opportunistic behaviors. Psychology explains the value function.

The value function shows us that the human being is risk averse, in the field of gains, and security-loving, in the field of losses. This behavior is easily observable in anonymous competitors participating in television competitions. For example, when most people are faced with the possibility of winning 100 thousand euros, with a probability of 25 percent or keeping the 15 thousand euros already won so far, a very large majority chooses not to play anymore. The expected value of 100 thousand euros multiplied by the probability of 25 percent, is 25 thousand euros, but the person chooses to keep the certain 15 thousand euros instead of trying to win the uncertain 100 thousand euros. Therefore, human beings are risk-averse in the field of earnings. However, in the domain of losses, human beings love security. Contrary to what happens in the domain of gains, whenever a person is given the possibility to pay to prevent harm from happening to him, he accepts paying more than the value resulting from neutrality in relation to risk. This is what happens, for example, with the insurance contract. The person is aware that the premium paid to the insurer is made up of the probability of occurrence of the claim multiplied by its probability of occurrence, to which a profit margin is subsequently added. But, in this case, the human being opts for a certain loss and buys the insurance contract, even if it has a higher expected value than what would result from the calculation of a neutral position toward the risk.

The value function

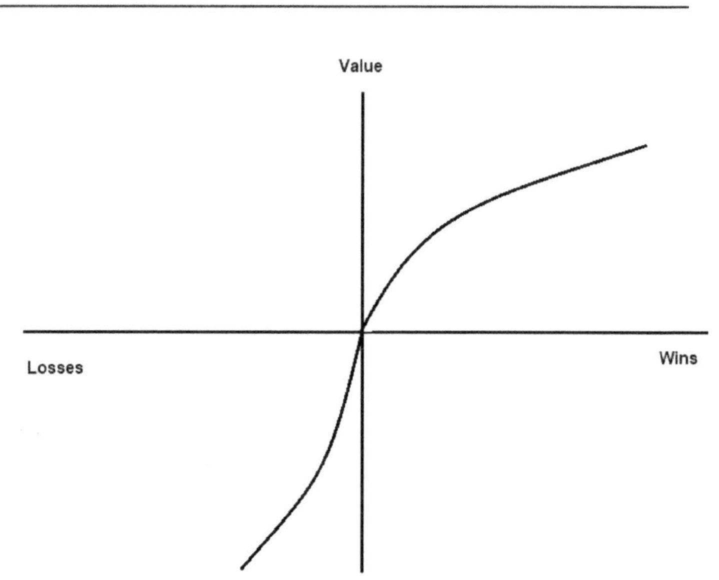

Note: Based on Kahneman, D. (2003) "A perspective on judgment and choice: mapping bounded rationality"

Psychology deepened this knowledge even further and explained that the slope of the function in the domain of gains is, from two to two and a half times, less inclined than what happens in the domain of losses. From the outset, the graphic sketch of the value function allows us to understand that the perception of the concepts of value, gain, penalty, and loss differs from individual to individual, depending on the circumstances in question. Thus, for a very rich person, who has an income of ten thousand euros per month, a fine of one hundred euros is felt in a completely different way from what happens with this same fine applied to a person who earns an income of only one thousand euros monthly.

The processes used by human beings to improve their living conditions assume a relative complexity, which extends beyond the intuitive thinking of the common mortal. In chess, the great players prepare traps through which they lure the opponent to start exchanging pieces that lead the player with greater depth of calculation to end up with an advantage on the board. Once they have the upper hand, these big players force the exchange of pieces of equal value – an action that is known as a simplification process. In the case of society in general, as a simplification process, we use money.

The use of money to facilitate trade between goods produced by members of a community is also the result of human evolution. Since the ancient times of societies of hunters, shepherds, and farmers, and during the periods of feudalism in the Middle Ages, people were allowed to work the land and make a living from it. Later, little by little, payment for the work done by people began to be done with goods such as meat, skins, wheat, corn, and salt. Salt was a rare commodity used by people to preserve food, especially meat. In this context, salt could pass from hand to hand without losing the properties for which it was appreciated by everyone. Gradually, in the second half of the fourteenth century, the practice of paying for human labor in exchange for salt was adopted, and the use of the term "salary" emerged to refer to the payment of labor by the owner of the resources.

The use of money, as an essential means for creating value, was irreproachably explained by Karl Marx, in 1867. The economist explained that the increase in the scale of industrial production allowed each producer to acquire control over such a volume of surplus that this would only be useful because it could be exchanged for the surpluses produced by other members of society. We can identify a process of creating value and improving the living conditions of the population that is based on the use of money to provide the exchange of goods. The commodity, "C," produced by a certain producer in large quantities, far beyond his consumption needs, is sold to his customers for money, "M." Subsequently, this producer uses the money he received to buy the commodity, "C", produced in surplus quantities by other members of society. Every society lives better because it makes available to its members a large number of goods that allow them to satisfy a greater number of needs. The "C-M-C" process, as referred to by Karl Marx, elucidates the importance of using money to improve the living conditions of populations. As money cannot be consumed, it thus acquires value for society due to its function as a facilitator of exchange. Money has exchange value only.

The above considerations on the notion of value are extremely important for the organization of humanity. We clearly see that a life of joy, happiness, and prosperity is based on the positive opportunistic behavior of community members. We also realize that society seeks to prevent negative opportunistic behavior from people by imposing penalties when their behavior deviates from what is legally recommended. However, the value of an option, which ultimately determines the decision of the human being, depends on the objective to be achieved and the circumstances in which the individual finds himself. When you live in a Pisistratus society type, which provides its members with more than what people need to be happy, and allows them to further improve their living conditions through commercial exchanges with other people, the application of fines on deviant behavior would be an effective and easy-to-apply mechanism, since society lives in a positive environment that rewards the effort of every human being. If we now look at the society of Genghis Khan, the application of the fine could only result in a reinforcement of the negative opportunistic behavior because the person could, for example, resort to new looting to pay the fine and still reap some increased, and immediate individual benefit, of their actions. The use of penalties loses effectiveness in a society where negative opportunistic behavior predominates. In any of the examples we have just given, society must have a control system over negative opportunistic behavior in order to achieve consistency in value creation. And the exercise of power assumes a decisive significance in the level of value that society manages to achieve.

Power

By definition, "power" means "to be able to". In the game of chess, the most powerful player is the one who has the ability to calculate, in greater depth, the consequences of his potential moves and, therefore, ends up winning his games. However, both players are entirely free to make their own decisions. Only the consequences of their decisions are different.

With regard to the consequences that come from each play, we can have, on the positive side, "brilliant, excellent, and good" plays, and, on the negative side, "blunders, mistakes, and inaccuracies." A "brilliant" move is one whose superiority over other options is only understood by the player who has great depth in chess thinking and can be absolutely decisive for winning the game. A move is "excellent" when it allows the simultaneous achievement of different strategic objectives of the game, affects the development of the opponent's game, and provides an advantageous position for the player who makes the decision. A "good" move is simply one that, while not having an impact as positive on the final result as a brilliant move or an excellent move, still contributes positively to the evolution of the pieces of that color on the board. On the negative side, a move is classified as a "blunder" when it immediately puts the player who made the decision at a sharp disadvantage in the game. A chess move is an "error" when it puts the player at a disadvantage on the board if the opponent manages to take advantage of the situation. Finally, the move is classified as an "inaccuracy" when a better-level player can identify more advantageous alternative moves, but the move that has just been executed, by itself, does not put the player at a significant disadvantage on the board. "Inaccuracy" always has a negative charge because the player who commits it loses the opportunity to make a play of positive value.

Having power means being free to do whatever you want. The chess player is free to make whatever decision he wants. But only the most competent player wins the game. The way power is exercised defines humanity's level of success.

In society, people only act in a certain way because they want to, and because they can. Both Pisistratus and Genghis Khan gained power by force and imposed their will on the rest of society. Seen from the perspective of a subject of those two dictators, power could be reduced to the ability that both had to subjugate others to their will. However, the exercise of power only becomes particularly relevant when, more than bending the other members of society to the whim of the powerful, it is able to consistently condition the behaviors that people end up adopting when following certain institutional rules.

The functioning rules of society defined by Pisistratus gave freedom of action to the citizens of Athens to take advantage of the opportunities they identified. Each Athenian could dedicate himself to agriculture, industry, transport, commerce, or the arts depending on the assessment he made of his abilities and the material resources available to him. Pisistratus used the fact of being able to condition the experience of Athenian society to encourage positive opportunistic behavior. These behaviors added more value the more they were replicated by other citizens. And the Athenians, mostly, acted in a certain way because they wanted to.

Genghis Khan's leadership took on a rather different frame. We can find reports that claim that the barbarian told his warriors several phrases consolidating the idea that the first, and only rule to be followed by his subjects, was to obey him. The behavior of people who were under his orders was thus guided by the lack of freedom. Even in battle, the action of each individual was perfectly restricted to the orders given to them by their direct commanders. It is said that punishments of flogging and death were instituted to ensure discipline in the ranks of his army. Each individual could only act in a certain way after being duly authorized. It is known that his soldiers were forbidden to practice any kind of looting on the conquered territories before the battles were won, which is an illuminating example of the lack of freedom that Genghis Khan granted to the members of his society. In this case, people behaved in accordance with the dictator's directives, not so much because they wanted to, but more because they had to.

Each individual in society can be consciously classified according to an analysis of the exercise of power he enjoys. Thus, for each person, we have four possible situations: the individual "wants and can;" the individual "does not want to and cannot;" the individual "does not want to and can;" and, finally, the individual "wants and cannot." A person is free when he "wants and can." In this case, each detected opportunity results in an action with consequences for society. A person is realistic when he "does not want to and cannot." No negative consequences result from this for society and no individual mistakes occur either. Now, society reaps the fruits of the organization it has when the situations in question are the last two. When the person "does not want to and can" we are in a situation where, in the eyes of the rest of society, the individual is considered in a derogatory way. The use of adjectives such as lazy or coward appears, which have this framework in the eyes of those who assume they are entitled to such an analysis. The tendency of the legislator, or the dictator, is to oblige the person to act in accordance with the guidelines of the powerful. The "lazy person," usually, is obliged to do what he is told. On the other hand, when the person "wants to and cannot," the individual is often called rebellious and undisciplined simply because he aspires to do things that the legislator understands not allow him to do. When a person is free and realistic, society reaches its maximum potential as long as people adopt positive opportunistic behaviors. When people adopt behaviors that qualify as laziness or rebellion, then we are facing clear situations of deficient institutional environments, in which a legislator forces members of society to act differently from what guides the interest of all people.

In chess, the greater harmony resulting from the sequence of moves decided by a player with greater depth of reasoning determines his success in relation to the opponent. In human society, the main determinant of our success is also the level of rationality that we manage to reach in the analysis of the rules that we build.

The exercise of power determines people's choices and, consequently, defines which opportunities are seized. How society is able to add value through the choice it makes between adopting opportunistic, positive, or negative, behaviors is easily illustrated by the behavior of lions in the African savannah.

In Africa, in a fertile territory, lived a pride of twelve lions. After the rainy season, vegetation in the area became abundant, and with it came large herds of zebras that began to graze in that area. Thousands and thousands of zebras came to enjoy those green lands. Behind the herds of zebra came a pride of six lions from another part of the savannah. When this new group of six lions entered the territory, they found a local lioness, who was alone and a few kilometers away from the rest of her group. The six lions, from the foreign group, killed the lioness, resident there, as soon as they saw her. From then on, the two groups of lions lived in constant disarray, hunting in the immense group of thousands of zebras that was available, but always subject to fights with lions belonging to another group than their own. The two groups together could have formed a community of eighteen lions that had thousands and thousands of zebras at their disposal that could last for eternity. Eighteen lions hunting in a group could choose the fattest, crunchiest, and most appetizing zebra they wanted. And none zebra would escape... Each hunt would be more productive and less tiring. They would feed at the desired time, had no failed hunts, and always choose the highest quality zebras. They would live in peace. The lions' inability to analyze the situation, combined with the difficulty in communicating effectively with each other, has brought the lions a huge opportunity loss regarding their overall welfare.

If we tried to classify the decisions made by the lions between "brilliant, excellent, or good," and "blunders, mistakes, or inaccuracies," it is certain that our analysis would lead us to conclude that the behavior of the lions is situated in this last line of reasoning. It is therefore important to understand the reason for the behavior of lions as deeply as possible.

Aware that animal behavior is primarily of an emotional nature, we can try to understand which emotions led to the lions' decision-making. The killing of the young lioness, by the second group of lions when they arrived in the new territory, reveals behavior led by fear. Consciously or unconsciously, every lion fears that one day the available zebras may not be enough for him. In this sense, greed is assumed to be an exacerbated expression of fear.

Greed is also a behavior identified in human beings and its justification is not always rationally perceived. The group of six lions, which killed the lioness that was alone, could not understand the global situation in which they found themselves and, even if they did, they would not be able to communicate with the lioness in the sense of defining a cooperation strategy. When fear is at the base of decision-making mechanisms, it is very difficult for the individual to establish an action plan that leads him to trust other members of the community. In these cases, the individual chooses to make his strength prevail, submitting others to his will. But the opportunity to improve the well-being of all, without exception, is lost.

Thus, the opportunity concept acquires a fundamental value to guarantee the quality of life of a community. The opportunity can only be considered by an individual when he is able to simultaneously assess the circumstances he is faced with and have the power to act in accordance with the reality he has just perceived. Each person can, therefore, act in order to immediately improve their well-being as long as they have the power to do so. The person wants, and can. The group of six lions attacked and killed the lioness who was alone because they believed that she would be less of an enemy to harm them, or less of a mouth to eat the zebras that grazed there. She was at mercy. And they had the power to carry out the decision they made given the available circumstances. In this case, the pride of lions engaged in a negative opportunistic behavior to the extent that this same action, if taken by elements of the other pride of lions, immediately contributes to worsening the well-being of the group itself. Cumulatively, by killing the lioness as soon as they saw her, they did not consider any kind of joint and coordinated action that could favor the global community of lions in the near future. They missed the opportunity to adopt a positive opportunistic behavior that would have allowed everyone to get better if the other elements of the community acted in the same way.

Power is, therefore, one of the main constraints on how society takes advantage of opportunities. The exercise of power is directly associated with the concept of value that the legislator embraces. And to the extent of the legislator's rationality as well. The success of a society is defined by the way in which these foundations are consolidated. The lions' attitude of competition for control of territory has an emotional basis rooted in fear. We know that emotions preside over decision-making before reason. We also know that the fear of loss is a feeling that is at least twice as intense as the desire for an equivalent gain. Thus, the competitive attitude emerges as an expression of the lower ability to reason, understand, and analyze the situation at hand, but which is induced by the animal's inability to control its own fear. On the other hand, only a very strong desire to aspire to a good life for himself and for all other members of the community, without exception, a desire that would have to overcome the fear of loss, could lead the dominant lions to a cooperative effort. Cooperation clearly emerges as the result of a greater capacity of the members of society for the correct exercise of power.

Economics identifies the economic game to highlight the advantage that cooperative behaviors acquire over competitive behaviors.

The economic game is illustrated through two players who can choose between two options: to compete or to cooperate. When someone chooses to compete, society achieves a total production of 10. When both choose to cooperate, the society achieves a total production of 12. The distribution of the society's total production between the two players is done as follows: 5-5, when both choose to compete; 7-3, when one player chooses to compete and the other chooses to cooperate; and 6-6, when both choose to cooperate. This game allows us to lay bare the bounds of our rationality.

Generally speaking, humans believe that we live in a competitive society. Additionally, people even believe that the success of a company or country lies in greater or lesser competitiveness. Looking at the economic game, we realize that reality is not like that. When we compete, we always miss the opportunity to reach higher levels of productivity through cooperation. Analyzing the economic game, we see that when both players agree to cooperate, but one of them enters into competition, then the traitor wins at first, with a result of 7 out of 10, and he is aware that he gets better than if he entered into cooperation because, at that point, he would manage to get a result of 6 out of 10. In this first analysis, the player has a clear incentive to enter into competition and deceive the opponent by pretending to be cooperative. However, the scam only lasts for one period. From then on, the other player, instead of cooperating, will compete forever. If we analyze the result, which both players obtain in four periods of the economic relationship, we realize that everyone loses when the chosen option is to compete. Effectively, suppose that, in the first period, "player 1" enters into the competition and deceives "player 2" who has committed to cooperating. In this case, after the first betrayal, "player 2" never agrees to cooperate again. After four periods, "player 1," who cheated first, has a cumulative result of 22, equal to 7+5+5+5, and "player 2" has a cumulative result of 18, equal to 3+5+5+5. If both players stick to the cooperation agreement, the score for both at the end of the four periods will be 24, equal to 6+6+6+6. As in the lions' case, here too all players lose out because they choose to adopt competitive attitudes.

But the analysis can be even further detailed when carried out under the emotional frame to which each player is subject. This analysis assumes great relevance since we know that emotions are processed by our brains before reason. And fear has a very significant weight in our decision-making process.

The economic game

		Player 2	
		To compete	To cooperate
Player 1	To compete	(5,5)	(7,3)
	To cooperate	(3,7)	(6,6)

Note: Result (Player 1, Player 2). Based on Rodrigues, J. C. (2022) "Virtuous economics"

The rationality of our mental positioning in society is thus under analysis. In the economic game, each participant is free to choose between cooperating with the other player, to obtain the highest possible production, or competing, to see who gets the most. Let us consider that "player 1" does not have the ability to assess the situation in the economic game from a perspective of continuity over time – just like a poor chess player who lacks depth in evaluating his moves. When "player 1" chooses to cooperate and "player 2" chooses to compete, "player 1" is aware that he loses 70% of the total production. He also realizes that he will always split the total production when he chooses to compete. So, "player 1," who is risk-averse and cannot assess the situation beyond the first period, will always choose to compete instead of cooperating, as this is the alternative that minimizes the risk of loss. Alternatively, if "player 1" is a person who wants to win regardless of what happens to the other player, then he is aware that he has two options: he cooperates to win 6 or he competes to keep 7. Naturally, taking into consideration the outcome of the first economic period only, the player who wants to win more always chooses to compete, as this is the option that maximizes the possibility of winning. It is, therefore, concluded that, regardless of the levels of ambition or risk aversion that each person has, the competitive attitude is just the result of the individual not being able to adequately consider the future consequences of his actions. A competitive society is a very bounded society in rational terms really.

We are in competition with ourselves. It is therefore

important to understand the "blunders, mistakes, and inaccuracies," and to identify the "brilliant, excellent, and good" moves. Today, in the middle of the 21st century, we begin to perceive the boundaries of our rationality and we need to grow through humility in order to recognize this. When power is properly exercised, the rules that condition the functioning of society induce positive opportunistic behavior. This, in turn, requires people to be free. When power is wielded incomprehensibly, the need to force obedience arises. In this situation, global productivity decreases, and humanity goes into decay. The quality of the exercise of power is a crucial element for the success of humanity.

This page was intentionally left blank.

Productivity

Productivity, power, and value are different concepts, but closely linked to each other. On the one hand, as mentioned before, "power" means "to be able to". On the other hand, the exercise of power only makes sense when it is intended to make the person feel good. Therefore, the exercise of power adds value to the decision-maker. An individual is productive when he is able to create value. The Dictionary of the Portuguese Language defines productivity as the quality of what is productive. Therefore, productivity is a measure of evaluation of an entity's ability to generate value for itself and others.

If we extend these important considerations to the whole society, it is difficult to understand what kind of value are we creating for us. Which society was more productive: the society of Pisistratus or the society of Temudjin? Which society brought the most value to humanity? The questions assume great relevance because the way each person defines their concept of value is a determinant of the given answer. But, adequately substantiating our answer is not an easy task

The exercise of power, in the sense of raising

productivity levels, implies increasing society's capacity to make the entire population feel good. As we saw earlier, we are always faced with the possibility of creating use value, exchange value, or both. We know that human beings positively value their ability to dedicate themselves to consumption and leisure. In 1776, when Adam Smith drew attention to the two concepts, both use value and exchange value were immediately related to the consumption of material goods. However, both extend to the immaterial realm and the way in which power is exercised, based on competitive or cooperative processes, will determine society's level of productivity.

In chess, a move is productive if it is "good, excellent, or brilliant" because it contributes positively to the player winning the game. But each move is conditioned by the rules of the game that the participants obey. And the decisions played are not always good.

In the year 2000, professor and economist Witold Henisz warned that people invest their resources in political activity when this is more profitable for them than economic activity. However, this type of investment does not contribute to increasing everyone's levels of well-being. Society is the more productive the greater the amount of value we are able to create for each other. The way in which the organization of society conditions the decisions of its members determines the levels of productivity, and well-being, that it is possible to achieve.

The game of chess is organized in a standard way. Defines a set of common rules, accepted by all players, letting each person evolve on the board as they see fit, through alternate moves. But each player is conditioned by the opponent's moves. And it is a greater understanding of this cause-consequence relationship that gives the best players an advantage.

Recognizing your opponent's worth and merit is absolutely crucial to winning a chess game. One of the first notions, to which the beginner in the study of chess is alerted, is to develop the habit of identifying the objective that the opponent wants to reach with the move he has just made. In this way, the player can prepare his next move according to his own attack objective, but without neglecting his defense.

In the game of chess, the rules are simple, well-defined, fully understood, and unanimously accepted by both players. In order to raise the productivity levels of our global society, in a serene and rational way, it is necessary to deepen our thinking in identifying the space that the rules grant for opportunistic, positive, and negative behaviors to manifest themselves.

The quest for productivity has taken on different forms over time. This evolution was masterfully explained, in 1776, by Adam Smith.

In the early days of *homo sapiens*, humanity survived exclusively by hunting. At that time, communities moved from one place to another, chasing their prey. The human genius was perfected and, with that, the creation and development of tools that facilitated the achievement of the objective took place. A multitude of hunting techniques, traps, and weapons were developed. Their knowledge was shared among the group members. Positive opportunistic behavior began to improve the living conditions of the hunting community. Simultaneously, each man was a hunter and a warrior. Each individual owned what he hunted. Additionally, each person realized that he could immediately improve his well-being by robbing others of their belongings. In making a decision, each man had to consider his actions as well as the possible reactions of other members of society. And each man also had to maintain himself, whether he was living in his territory or when he was out fighting his enemies. Society was not conveniently organized to efficiently guarantee the needs of food and defense among themselves.

Based on the understanding of these shortcomings, the man began to ensure control of his own food through the creation and control of herds of animals, sheep, and goats. Pastoral communities emerged. As in the society of hunters, societies of shepherds also had to move from one place to another, in harmony with the available pastures. However, this time, when the community moved, it moved together and held all its members together. The actions, of food and defense, became collective tasks. Animal herds became a common resource. Then, human society began to gain efficiency in coordinating the efforts of all people. The shepherd society reached superior living conditions to the hunter society. The latter made its survival dependent on the individual ability to find prey in the wild, while the pastoral society came to have direct control over its own global diet. Consequently, pastoral societies easily conquered hunter-societies.

But human ingenuity continued to persist in identifying opportunities that could lead to an improvement in the population's living conditions and agricultural techniques were developed. These techniques, in addition to the control of animal feeding, also allowed the control of reinforcing plant feeding, both for humans themselves and to improve the quality of their herds. Then came the society of farmers. Now, the community lived in a fixed location and could no longer move outside to be at war with the enemy. Even so, between the sowing and harvesting periods, there was a period of agricultural growth that allowed them to go to other territories to plunder, and steal, the belongings of other communities. When at war, each farmer had to support himself. Thus, the effectiveness of their coordinated efforts was necessarily confined to the time period inherent in the growth of crops.

But the human genius continued to manifest itself and its positive effects were reflected in the welfare of society. Metal handling techniques were developed. The most varied tools to facilitate human work were invented. Arts and economic activities indirectly related to each other were developed. Professions such as blacksmith, welder, shoemaker, carpenter, or weaver arose. At this point, it became impossible to entice these professionals to go to war because that meant forcing these people to give up their only source of livelihood, exchanging certainty for uncertainty. From then on, those who went to war had to be supported by the general public. Improvements in the war effort required increasing industrial development, and soldiers were maintained by the efforts of all non-soldiers. In this way, the percentage of the community devoted to the war effort became increasingly small.

Until this stage of humanity's progress, we clearly identified how the affectation of the members of a community was happening over time. The increasing use of tools that facilitate human work allowed agricultural productivity to increase and the same amount of food became possible to obtain with fewer hours of work. Due to this fact, people were progressively relocated to where they were most needed. In other words, fewer and fewer people were assigned to agricultural activities, and in return, more and more people were concentrated on industrial activities.

At this point in the development of human society, Adam Smith once again alerted us to the essence of human behavior. With great mastery, the economist tells us the story of a boy who worked in a factory. The boy had direct intervention in the operation of one of the first steam engines designed by man. The child's intervention was limited to alternately opening and closing the communication between the boiler and the cylinder, as the piston rose or fell. The child wanted to go play with his friends instead of being tied to that factory activity. At a certain point, the child realized that he could tie a string, joining the handle of the valve that opened the communication between the boiler and the cylinder, causing the machine to start working without his help and leaving him free to go and play with his friends. One of the most important inventions that human genius conceived for the improvement and development of the steam engine was the result of the desire of a boy who wanted to have time to play.

In its simplest essence, the human being needs to have conditions for consumption and leisure. And each person seeks to use society's operating rules to reach the highest levels of both.

In the book "The Wealth of Nations", in 1776, Adam Smith used the metaphor of an "invisible hand" that naturally led society to raise its quality of life. The author explained that society can raise its levels of well-being if it grants freedom of action to its citizens. He realized that each human being, in pursuit of individual goals of profit, would dedicate himself to taking advantage of the opportunities within his reach to satisfy the needs of others. Thus, an entrepreneur would successively create new production units whenever he saw the opportunity to produce something that would simultaneously bring benefits to himself and the rest of the community. Adam Smith stressed the importance of individual freedom for a society to be productive. And he explained how fostering rules that guarantee freedom of action can lead to prosperity.

The action of the "invisible hand" depends directly on the rules on which society accepts to evolve. Each entrepreneur will try to produce the goods that the rest of society needs with the aim of selling these products at the highest possible price. Maximum profit is thus defined as the difference between the price that other members of society are willing to pay for the product and the production cost that the entrepreneur has to bear to produce those goods or services. This results in two consequences. First, the maximum price at which the producer can sell his goods or services is always defined by the demand directed at him by the other members of society. If the seller asks for an exchange price above what society is willing to pay, he will not be able to sell his product. Second, the profit dimension signals to all members of society which activities are most valued. So, for example, if the production of electricity is a very profitable activity, then society needs more people to dedicate themselves to this activity so that the quantities available to everyone increase, and these are sold at a lower price. This action will be increasing until the available quantities of the good are as high as possible and its price is as low as possible. Inevitably, this reality means that the commercialization of that product reaches a situation of zero profit and society is able to maximize the salary of all the people who participate in that productive activity, employers and employees, guaranteeing the maximum global prosperity that is possible to obtain with the available technology and resources.

The concept of productivity thus takes on three different forms.

Let us first consider the case of the entrepreneur. The producer considers that his activity is productive if it allows him to generate a high amount of profit. The person has created a use value equal to the cost of producing the good but intends to obtain an additional gain for himself by exchanging it for a much higher value. The profit obtained from selling his product will allow him to purchase as many goods as possible produced by the other members of the community. For the entrepreneur, he is the more productive the greater his capacity to be a monopolist in selling his product to society.

Second, we have to consider the notion of productivity from the employee's perspective. The work efforts developed by the employee provide him with a salary. With this salary, the person will satisfy his consumption needs and, like Adam Smith's boy who tied the string between the boiler and the cylinder, this individual also aspires to have more free time for himself. From the employee's perspective, his productivity is all the greater as the simultaneous amounts of salary and free time are at his disposal. It is important to note that this feeling extends to the employer, who is always an employee of his own.

Third, we identify the productivity of society. Society is productive when it is capable of generating the highest levels of well-being for all, using as little of the available resources as possible. This means that society is productive when it produces as many goods and services as possible, at the lowest possible price, making people work as little time as possible. This necessarily means that a society maximizes its productivity when the profit on traded goods and services is nil and people are permanently at full employment.

Over the centuries, the sharing of knowledge has allowed us to evolve towards a situation of increasing specialization of human activity. The simultaneity between ever-increasing levels of specialization and sharing of know-how meant that a smaller and smaller percentage of the population was able to dedicate itself to agriculture – while this being sufficient to ensure food for the entire community. First, it was possible to replace the hoe with the plow. Afterward, we managed to replace the plow with the tractor. In the same line of reasoning, to ensure that we have at our disposal the material goods we need, it is now necessary to have a smaller and smaller proportion of people involved in industrial activity. In this way, the growing number of available people in the active population ends up dedicating themselves to service activities. The provision of services is the maximum exponent of the focus of economic activity on the production of well-being for the other members of society and the development of entertainment activities has acquired increasing importance. The construction of a prosperous society is based on the individual capacity that each human being has to put their knowledge and talents at the service of the community.

But this understanding of the virtuous collective functioning of a society does not find strong bases in our individual rationality. As human beings, because we use money to facilitate exchanges, we easily confuse the concepts of use value and exchange value. On an individual basis, and as a result of our lesser ability to deepen our reasoning, we record negative opportunistic behaviors, which lead the entire population to live worse if replicated by the other members of society. The employer often tends to seek to create conditions to be a monopolist. Employees tend to adopt "social loafing" attitudes; that is, the person takes advantage of the fact of being part of a workgroup to reduce his productive efforts. And it is still frequent to see individual behaviors that aim to emphasize the power of a fraction of society over the rest. There are several examples of the pressure that is exerted on the governments of each country to create rules that favor the sectoral interests of a small portion of society. On the one hand, actions are developed to create barriers to the entry of competition in a given economic activity. Some examples of violations of the free functioning of the market are the use of customs barriers, the obligation to obtain formal licenses in advance before deploying a business, the obligation to meet a large number of requirements in order to be able to carry out an economic activity, the definition of a maximum number of vacancies for entry into universities to learn certain courses, etc, etc, etc. On the other hand, there are protests, strikes, and the use of all imaginable means to manage to safeguard the highest wages, working as little as possible. People resort to an extensive range of expedients that allow the strength of an individual, or of a fraction of society, to prevail over the other members of the community. We enter into a competition. We focus on the extent of the consequences of our actions in the very short term. We are not able to properly assess the reactions that will follow, nor the global consequences for our individual well-being. There is a behavioral tendency to allow ourselves to be conditioned by our bounded rationality, while realizing that, similarly to what happens in chess, it is through the alternate exercise of each move that we have to seek to achieve an advantageous position on the board. And in our case, regrettably, every move has been perpetrated by attempting to manipulate the rules of the game.

As in chess, so in Economics, the use of mathematical models is solely intended to materialize simple ideas that try to represent the truth of facts and evaluate possibilities of action. One of the simplest and most interesting economic models, which helps to understand why society reaches certain levels of productivity depending on its operating rules, was published by Timothy Besley and Maitreesh Ghatak, in 2010. The authors developed an economic model, which is a peaceful translation of reality into mathematical functions, and allows for an expeditious explanation of the main determinants of the levels of productivity that a society can achieve.

The model developed by the two authors is based on four basic assumptions: 1) it assumes that people positively value consumption and leisure capabilities; 2) assumes that society is made up of a producer individual and a non-producer individual; 3) assumes that the individual producer has a property from which he can extract a consumer good through his work effort; and 4) it assumes that the amount of goods produced by the producer, per hour of work, is decreasing over time – that is, the income from work decreases with the number of hours of work performed, due to the effect of fatigue. It is, therefore, important to enable the model of dynamic evolution and understand its effects.

Considering the existence of growing tiredness as the person increases his dedication to work, it is easily perceived that there is an optimal amount of work that allows the producer to obtain a certain amount of the good he produces and a given allocation of free time, which he also values. This optimal combination of work and leisure is the one that brings the greatest satisfaction to the producer.

However, the other individual in this model society, who lacks the means of production, also needs to consume the good. And this need has consequences for the functioning of the society. Thus, a part of the total production, the fruit of the producer's work, is somehow expropriated by the non-producer individual. This form of expropriation can be the result of social pressure for the producer to make a donation, it can be through the use of taxes, or through theft, pure and simple. Whatever the form of expropriation verified, the end result is that the producer is left with a smaller amount of the good available to him, without obtaining, in return, any increase in his free time. In this way, the optimum production level of the producer is reduced. The latter starts to dedicate a smaller proportion of his time to the production of the good and to dedicate a greater part of his time to his leisure activities. Economics thus uses a simple mathematical model to prove something that is even quite intuitive: the greater the level of expropriation to which the result of work effort is subject, the less the work effort that the individual will commit to producing a given good. Society is as productive as its ability to meet the needs of all its members, without exception.

This fact explains the importance of safeguarding private property rights for economic prosperity. The individual producer will be all the more committed as the guarantee he has that his work efforts will be duly rewarded. However, he is not alone in society and this situation forces the owner of the means of production to consider some possibilities. These possibilities will be all the more extended the greater the number of individuals that exist in society and who are devoid of means of production of that good. On the one hand, to minimize the effect of expropriation, the producer can hire some people to guard the result of his production, sharing part of the income from his work, paying for the protection service, and controlling the expropriation factor to which he is subject. On the other hand, the producer can seek to increase his production by resorting to the work of the individual who does not own the means of production, but who can help him to produce more, in the same period of time. In this way, the total production achieved by society can be distributed among all its members, who share the work effort among themselves and use the human and material resources at their disposal in a more rational way.

In the latter case, the individual who does not have material properties will also evaluate the possibility of dedicating time and effort to the work proposed by the producer, holder of private property. The person considers the possibility of becoming an integral part of the production process with the right to a part of the total income of his work. This worker also gets tired and positively values his leisure time too. This individual, employed by the producer, is aware of what he is capable of producing. Thus, if a significant part of the income from his work remains in the possession of his employer, then the individual's optimal effort is reduced. This is exactly the same intuitive reasoning as it happens to the producer when he is expropriated of his assets: an employee is more productive the lower the value of his production that is expropriated by his employer. In other words, a person who works for others will be more productive the closer his salary is to the value of the good or service that the individual produces, and that is firstly in the possession of his employer.

Society's productivity depends, therefore, on safeguarding a set of global rules that function in dependent articulation. The effects of this articulation are positive when extending its application to all members of society, allowing the highest possible level of well-being to be achieved. However, whenever negative opportunistic behavior manifests itself, the effects of this articulation cause a decline in society's levels of well-being. Society only becomes truly productive when it learns to inhibit negative opportunistic behavior while encouraging positive opportunistic behavior.

As the excellent chess player does, the success of

society requires a depth of reasoning that extends beyond the short term, without neglecting the fact that, immediately, we have to be attentive to the opponent's move. It is, therefore, crucial to understand how a certain chain of action-reaction situations will determine the behavior of all members of society, without exception.

Continuing with the simple employer-employee model, let us define the employer as the entity that determines the operating rules of his company, which all employees must obey. The rules are defined by the employer in order to obtain the maximum possible productivity. Let us assume that the employer wants to eradicate all kinds of mistakes made by employees because the mistakes result in an increase in the cost of production borne by his company. Let us also assume that the cost of an error is greater the later it is detected. Finally, let us assume that the salaries to be paid to employees have a fixed amount. So, given these three assumptions, given that the selling price is defined by the market, that is, by the maximum value at which the producer perceives that he can sell the product to his customers, and the production costs are perfectly defined, the errors committed by employees are seen by the employer as an immediate reduction in his potential profit. Since the employer wants to eliminate or reduce the occurrence of errors to the furthest extent, he needs to detect the existence of errors as soon as possible.

The scenario proposed above has an effective proximity to the real need of companies in the early detection of production errors. In this context, the employer can define two different types of rule systems to achieve this objective: a system based on the use of the penalty, or a system based on the use of the reward. The penalty-based system is based on the legislator's perception of the effect of fear on decision-making. Human beings are willing to pay more than necessary to avoid the possibility of a greater loss. On the other hand, the reward-based system is based on the understanding that the person is risk-averse. The human being prefers to have a certain gain to an uncertain one. The effectiveness of the two systems in driving each individual's behavioral choices is thus under scrutiny.

Starting with a penalty-based system of rules, the employer can define that it does not admit more than three errors in a given period of time. The rule can be defined as follows: "If more than three errors occur during a month, the employee will be dismissed with just cause." The legislator seeks to oblige the employee to be aware of errors while avoiding them at all costs. With the adoption of this type of rule, the legislator shows that he abhors errors and seeks productivity. However, this rule induces each employee who makes a mistake to hide the mistake from the employer in order to avoid being fired after the third error, either by hiding processes or by imputing the blame to someone else. Another consequence of this rule for the employer is that he obliges himself to create error detection mechanisms, which always result in increased costs. To be effective, the penalty-based system requires full employee compliance with the rules implemented by the legislator. However, due to the response it inevitably receives from those targeted by the rules, its effectiveness is necessarily limited by the supervisory capacity that the employer is able to build. The regulatory system, based on penalty, is based on fear. In the fear that the legislator has that mistakes happen and in the fear that the legislator seeks to impose on the targets of the rule regarding the consequences of their non-compliance. This system, by itself, does not encourage positive opportunistic behavior. And it is quite fallible when it comes to inhibiting negative opportunistic behavior.

Another approach, available to legislators to encourage their employees to eradicate errors, is to offer a reward for each error reported to the employer. The rule can be defined as follows: "For each error identified by the employee who committed it, the company will pay ten euros." This rule allows the employer to detect errors as early as possible and does not need a fierce supervisory system to be successful. But the employer is acting positively, confident that his employees do everything to avoid mistakes, although aware that mistakes do happen. This rule is not intuitive. Apparently, the creation of a rule that compensates for the error, instead of promoting its eradication, will rather foster its proliferation. In this situation, the employee now has a clear incentive to report every mistake he made to the employer as soon as possible. We clearly understand that if the employee decides to act in the negative mode, he will make deliberate mistakes to receive an additional ten euros for each one. Now, after compensating his employees for the positive opportunistic behavior of early identification of the error, the employer can create the second rule, which safeguards him against the possibility that they will try to take advantage of his goodwill by creating the first rule. This second rule is as follows: "An employee who makes more than three mistakes in a month can be dismissed with just cause." This is the same rule as the penalty-based system, and at first glance, it looks like it will have the same end result. An employee who wants to maximize his profitability now has a clear incentive to make three mistakes in the month, receive the thirty euros, and, from then on, hide his mistakes. Once again, it seems that the company that adopts the reward-based system can only get worse. Therefore, the legislator's positive stance requires the definition of a third rule: "The employee who has no errors during the month will receive forty euros." Checkmate! Now, all company employees have a real and consistent incentive to avoid mistakes, reporting them to their employer as soon as they detect them. They earn another ten euros for every error detected. They earn another forty euros a month if they work without errors. In this example, only the fourth error will always tend to be hidden by employees. Creating a reward-based regulatory system is the most effective way to achieve the two goals of inhibiting negative opportunistic behavior and stimulating positive opportunistic behavior. The members of this community acquire the habit of acting positively, not because the supervision forces them to do so, but because they know that everyone has a positive reason for doing so. So the members of this society learn to trust each other.

Human societies usually impose fear-based regulatory systems on their members. Mechanisms are created that hinder positive opportunistic behavior and translate into the development of huge inhibiting bureaucracies. Fear sometimes gets in the way. In 1981, Oliver Williamson, Nobel Prize in Economics in 2009, recognized that the creation of government structures and mediation of commercial practices for goods and services was necessary to harmonize economic relations between the parties. Building rules that inhibit negative opportunistic behavior was then identified as a need for productive societies. Later, in 1994, in the annual report of the famous American company General Electric, Jack Welch, the chairman of the board of directors of the company at the time, complained that it had been possible to identify documents where ten signatures were needed to get something done. A huge inhibiting bureaucracy had been created! In most of these situations, the legislator fails to be aware of the global range of consequences inherent in forcing a certain rule. In the same line of reasoning, a garden bench is no longer used… And the chimpanzees end up hitting each other without being able to explain why!

Bases of regulatory systems: Penalty versus Reward

<u>Penalty:</u>

1° "If more than three errors occur during a month, the employee will be dismissed with just cause"

<u>Reward:</u>

1° "For each error identified by the employee who committed it, the company will pay ten euros"

2° "If more than three errors occur during a month, the employee will be dismissed with just cause"

3° "The employee who has no errors during the month will receive forty euros"

Note: Example of possible rule sets for early detection of production errors and their correction.

When trying to implement reward-based regulatory systems, the difficulty increases a lot for the legislator. The use of power in a negative sense is relatively easier, and likely, because it is an expression of fear. It's an emotional reaction. And we know that emotions plague our minds before reason. In turn, acting in a positive sense requires greater effort and rational thinking from the legislator. It is more demanding in terms of the depth of reasoning it requires and still frequently encounters the dissatisfaction of those who have not yet managed to understand the integrated way in which the rules operate with each other. Implementing reward-based regulatory systems is an expression of legislator courage.

It is important to note that the three rules identified above, which the legislator used to create a regulatory system based on reward, only make sense when used together. It is also essential to emphasize that each rule was created sequentially, after realizing the response returned by the negative opportunistic behavior that the first and second rules stimulated. However, the legislator's choices were always guided by the reward of positive opportunistic behavior. A society that bases its rules on reward-based systems is a more productive society because it manages to achieve higher levels of production of goods and services at a lower cost. It is this deepening of our reasoning in identifying possible action-reaction sequences that lead to the consolidation of economic and social development.

Resorting to the use of fully accepted rules is paramount to the success of humanity. It has been through the development of virtuous laws that economic progress has taken place. Good, honest, just, and noble laws, which bring well-being to the whole society, need to be trusted. To be reliable, society's operating rules cannot be constantly changing depending on the faction that decides to change them. As in chess, the rules must be the same for everyone and each person must be able to freely choose how to make moves according to the established rules. Prior acceptance of rules that serve everyone's interests is crucial. But there can only be universal acceptance of the rules when we all understand why we should play the game that way. Virtuous laws, which optimize society's productivity, will only be accepted on a global scale when they are capable of exercising effective control over the emotional reactions triggered by fear. And only then does society maximize its productive potential.

Fear of loss

The effects of fear on chess players' decision-making process are laid bare by the game. In particular, there are two types of checkmate that chess students learn when they take their first steps in the game: the "épaulettes" mate and the "muffled" mate. Briefly, the "épaulettes" mate consists of taking advantage of the fact that the opponent is so afraid of losing the king that he tries to protect it, on both sides, with the two rooks. The rooks thus function as jambs designed to protect the king. However, when under threat, the positioning of the rooks removes mobility and escape options from the king. And the opponent takes advantage of this situation by creating a checkmate. On the other hand, the "muffled" mate is based on the same concept. The situation of checkmate is provoked by taking advantage of an identical situation, in which our opponent is so afraid of losing the king that he will surround it with a large number of pieces of his color, but these end up taking away from the king any possibility of escaping in the face of our attack on his current position. Fear takes away human discernment.

Our behavior in society is identical. First, we protect

our king so much that we neglect other key pieces. Secondly, we are usually unable to use the full potential of the pieces at our disposal. Finally, we place ourselves at the mercy of a checkmate even before the opponent poses an effective danger to our king. We are so afraid of war, hunger, disease, financial chaos, loss of wages, and so many other unpleasant situations that we end up creating conditions for them to become a reality. As with the successful chess player, controlling fear is imperative for a happy society that realizes its full potential.

Our global society is organized around four main cornerstones: families, firms, government, and the financial system. Generally speaking, business, government, and the financial system exist to create the necessary conditions of production, security, and commerce that allow families to live as well as possible. We have already realized that the productivity of society stems from what it is capable of giving to itself. Therefore, assuming that humanity intends to safeguard the best living conditions for all its members, then why is full employment not guaranteed to the entire population?

The issue becomes particularly sensitive when we realize that it is something quite easy to achieve. Indeed, we can employ all people with the capacity to work as long as we want to do so. Solutions may involve reducing working hours, increasing the duration of vacation periods, retiring people earlier, a combination of the previous three, or another panoply of possible solutions that allow achieving this virtuous objective.

We know that the fear of loss takes priority in the decision process. We also know that its intensity is fearsome. Therefore, society has an effective need to understand what are the fears that manifest themselves in individual decision-making and that condition the levels of collective well-being that it manages to achieve.

In the eighteenth century, at the beginning of the development of classical economic theory, very much based on the confidence in the success of the "invisible hand" of Adam Smith, and on the ideas of "laissez-faire, laissez-passer" of Jacques Turgot, global society consolidated its functioning around the defense of private property and the stimulus to entrepreneurship. In general terms, this economic theory advocates that freedom of action in the market by entrepreneurs will result in the creation of more and more firms. These, in turn, will lead to the creation of more jobs. This conducts to an improvement in the purchasing conditions of the general population and, therefore, an improvement in the living conditions of society as a whole. However, when these pillars are built in society, people develop the most varied opportunistic, positive, and negative behaviors. And fear expresses its strength.

In 1936, in his book "The General Theory of Employment, Interest, and Money," John Maynard Keynes explained two fundamental concepts of today's society: 1) why there is involuntary unemployment in an economy; and 2) why people hold cash in their possession.

The author explained that involuntary unemployment in the economy is an inevitability in today's society. According to classical theory, based on the development of positive opportunistic behaviors, the continuous activity of entrepreneurs in exploiting lucrative business opportunities constitutes a natural process of progressive reduction of profit in the most varied economic sectors, at the same time that progress is made toward the total employment of the active population. But as more and more people are employed, the higher wage demanded by employees is paid by employers. Employers' profits are getting smaller and smaller. Thus, their propensity to continue investing also decreases, as the lucrative opportunities identified in the market are reduced. When fear of the future sets an uncertainty affecting entrepreneurs' security and the estimated profitability of the ventures is no longer attractive, people withdraw their investment intentions and the situation of full employment is hardly achieved.

Keynes also explained that individuals hold money for three different reasons: 1) for the transaction reason, to exchange among themselves the goods they produce; 2) for the precautionary reason, to face the uncertainty that the future holds; and 3) for the speculation reason, because they believe they are better prepared than the market to take advantage of a given circumstance.

The economist verified, empirically, that people increase the proportion of their savings when their income increases, holding a proportionately larger amount of their income to face the uncertainty that the future represents. In this way, the proportion of income that is consumed decreases as the percentage of employed people increases in society. As a result, some companies are no longer able to sell all of their production and are forced to lay off employees or reduce wages. These two solutions are firmly rejected by workers as, in fact, they constitute a worsening of their living conditions. But this rejection only sharpens the employers' response. Therefore, under the current functioning rules of global society, the situation of full employment will always be a level of well-being that society rarely reaches, but if it does, the situation will inevitably be ephemeral.

We are in a position to identify some fears that condition society's ability to reach higher levels of well-being. They are the fear of losing profit and the fear of losing wages. But these two fears are emotions detected as a result of the unique interaction between employers and employees. They are stimulated by the functioning of the institutional environment in which people find themselves. But society is also made up of members of the government and the financial system, and the actions of employers and employees have direct consequences on the decision-making processes of both government officials and bankers.

Both the government and the financial system are key players for human society to win the game. The government can define the rules that encourage positive opportunistic behavior, inhibit negative opportunistic behavior, and determine the improvement, or worsening, of the living conditions of populations. The financial system, in addition to being crucial as an element that facilitates the exchange of goods and services, either through the provision of means of payment services or through the opening of lines of credit for investment, is also decisive in encouraging the private initiative of those who do not have the means of production and intend to acquire them from other producers who are making less use of the productive means available to them. Thus, when banks grant credit for the installation of new production units, they are decisive in promoting competition between entrepreneurs. And they are also making a fundamental contribution so that society can have a greater quantity of goods at lower prices. It is therefore important to understand what are the fears that affect these economic agents and that prevent them from rising to guarantee the creation of a society that lives permanently in full employment.

After Keynes demonstrated that, under the current rules of operation, the private sector of the economy could never permanently guarantee a situation of full employment, the society acquired a general acceptance that it would be up to the public sector to assume this function. Throughout the 20th century, in the most varied ways, but generally on a global scale, human society developed institutional models aimed at maintaining the income of all members of society. As a result, governments began to determine relatively rigid rules to prevent redundancies from arising, to prevent wages from being reduced, and to guarantee that people have jobs, even if it is in the civil service. The public sector has assumed a decisive role in the success of the private sector. On the one hand, the government ensures the creation of crucial infrastructure for the development of entrepreneurship. The creation of power stations, the development and generalization of communications, and the promotion of means of transport are some virtuous examples of the public sector's contribution to the success of the private sector. On the other hand, the government ensures the purchasing power of a part of the population, which is directed to products produced by private companies. But the government also has to secure its revenues. It has to do one of two things: 1) either charge for the services it provides to the community – and then it acts as if it were a private company; and 2) or it collects taxes from the population – which it then uses as it sees fit to finance the activities under its responsibility. Often, to avoid situations of tax increases at a given time, and with the intention of deferring this inevitability into the future, the governments of the most diverse countries choose to contract debt with private banking. The conditions are thus created for the root of fear to flourish.

If a government wants to guarantee, permanently, the situation of full employment to its population, this will have to be assured by the private sector or by the public sector. If it is ensured by the public sector, then, when society reaches full employment and people start to save proportionally more to face the uncertainty that the future holds, reducing the aggregate demand directed to the products of private companies, the government, necessarily, will have to lower wages, reduce the number of civil servants or increase tax collection even more. In either situation, the government will be contested by the population. On the other hand, as we have already seen, the productivity of society is greater the smaller the value of private enterprise production that is expropriated. And any increase in taxes necessarily leads to lower productivity in the economy. In this case, despite being aware that society is not as productive as it could be in a full-employment situation, the government opts for the non-optimal situation, trying to make it minimally satisfactory for as many people as possible, given the circumstances. Cumulatively, wage rigidity, combined with the comfortable maintenance of jobs, encourages less work effort on the part of employees without employers being able to effectively reverse the situation. The fear of loss of productivity combines with the fear of loss of popularity and, together, they induce the government to accept the existence of involuntary unemployment in society.

However, if the government enacts the full-employment society, whether guaranteed exclusively by private companies, whether guaranteed by private companies, and by government companies acting as private companies, then it would make no sense to levy taxes. In this case, each service provided by a public company would have the appropriate price, according to what the market allows. The government would lose the ability to collect the taxes it sees fit. And today, most of the world's governments have a public debt to the private banks of other countries. Thus, in the short term, the government that opts for optimizing the productivity of its society faces three additional fears: 1) the fear of fiscal redundancy, as the collection of taxes ceases to make sense and the loss of control over that certain revenue can be frightening; 2) the fear of not being able to service the debt if the general public opts for the services of private companies other than those of the government; and 3) the fear of having to explain these possibilities to their population and not being understood. Faced with the strength and intensity of these fears, the governments of most countries choose not to guarantee full employment to their populations.

Like governments, despite not having direct active participation in the production of goods and services, the action of the financial system is also decisive for economic and social progress for three fundamental reasons. First, banks provide the means of payment that allow exchanges of produced surpluses to take place. Second, banks provide the service of safekeeping for the savings of those who want to consume part of their present income in the future. And third, banks provide the credit that allows a private entity to engage in the acquisition of the productive means it needs to develop economic activity. As any service company does, banks also exchange their product for other goods and services produced in society. But in addition to providing services, banks also produce money. And they are the only economic agent with the power to do so.

It is the harmonious development of these four parts of society – families, firms, government, and banks – that leads society to success. However, the creation of institutional rules that determine wage, labor, and tax rigidity will define the possible choices so that opportunistic, positive, and negative behaviors can take place. These can originate economic and social balances or imbalances. It is the result of the interaction of these choices that defines the level of well-being that any society can achieve.

In the specific case of banks, the production of money constitutes revenue that does not involve any commercial exchange. Consequently, the institutional rule that allows this production introduces an imbalance in the functioning of society. And this is a revenue that banks are not willing to do without. It is, therefore, necessary to understand how the creation of a full-employment society disrupts the ability of banks to continue producing money.

Suppose that society decides to create a fixed initial endowment of money and that this is given into the hands of all those who own productive means. Let us further assume that banks cannot create money to extend credit. Employers will then use this money to hire workers while paying them a salary to do so. Workers will deposit this salary in the bank and the bank charges commissions in exchange for providing the means of payment and safekeeping service to its customers. With these commissions, the bank will consume the goods and services produced by firms. With the money from their salary, workers will consume the goods available in the economy and save a part for future consumption. Finally, banks lend money from workers' savings to employers looking to start new businesses. In the future, this money will be returned by the entrepreneurs, leaving the bank with a commission for the financial intermediation service. In this scenario, banks are a private sector firm that exchanges its services with other private sector firms. Nothing disturbs the normal functioning of society as long as credit-financed businesses are successful and debtors comply with the future repayment of the value of the savings made by workers.

In the scenario just identified, the creation of a full-employment society raises several fundamental problems. First, if the entrepreneur, instead of investing in the creation of a new business uses the workers' savings to consume himself, in the present, a value that goes beyond his income, then, in the future, this entrepreneur will not be able to refund the value of this savings if it maintains the same consumption pattern. The worker is expropriated from his savings, his expectations are frustrated and he loses confidence in the financial sector. In this case, the fear of loss on the part of the worker will lead him to avoid depositing his salary in the bank. The positive function of the bank for the functioning of society loses effectiveness. Second, faced with the scenario of a full-employment economy, and with the entrepreneur considering the possibility of starting a new business, the most effective way at his disposal to attract the employees he needs is to pay them a salary higher than what people already earn working for the competition. Attracting good competitors' employees by paying higher wages can only be done at the cost of sacrificing the investor's profits. And, in this case, the opportunities that an ordinary worker detects to get involved in entrepreneurship will be much smaller. On the one hand, lucrative investment opportunities for entrepreneurs are closed. On the other hand, entrepreneurs are aware that the only way within their reach to enjoy good employees is by resorting to those in competition or by increasing the salaries paid to the best employees they already have at home. Both cases imply a loss of profit. The fear of losing profit on the part of entrepreneurs, and the fear of losing income on the part of bankers, will make both oppose the creation of a full-employment society. Third, the workers, aware that it is the owners of the means of production who simultaneously determine the wages to be paid and the selling price of the products produced, realize that society can maintain a low average wage level while imposing high prices for the products they need. Workers, therefore, have to live a reality of meager living conditions. Once again, in this scenario, the fear of losing wage is manifested, and workers also rise up against the implementation of a full-employment society.

However, in this scenario that we have just seen, where banks cannot create money, there is a positive safeguard that society has. We will be facing a situation in which each family has a certain family budget to spend on available products. Each entrepreneur puts his products on sale at the highest price he can and tries to keep the wages of his workers as low as possible. Thus, employers play the economic game competitively and keep the highest possible value that can be immediately removed from total production. Given that family budgets are perfectly defined, whenever an entrepreneur decides to increase the sale price of his products, one of two things will happen: either the entrepreneur cannot sell; or, being a basic necessity, other entrepreneurs will only be able to sell the same quantities of their goods if they lower their selling price. When banks do not create money, regardless of the level of wages paid, society can always ensure that there is no inflation. There may be fluctuations in the prices of the basket of products available, but there cannot be a generalized rise in prices. When banks do not create money, inflation is eradicated.

But, contrary wise to what the scenario presented above assumed, the truth is that banks create money. The creation of money by banks provides them with a set of important faculties: 1) it reduces, and may even eliminate, the need to pay interest on workers' savings – be they employers or employees; 2) allows banks to be partners in new businesses; 3) allows banks to finance consumer credit operations; 4) allows banks to lend money to governments; and 5) it allows banks to create inflation. How a full-employment society might affect these powers is always a concern for the financial system.

Given that banks can create money to lend to entrepreneurs whenever they detect a good business opportunity, banks have a clear incentive not to remunerate workers' savings. As banks will create lines of credit with new money, they do not have to remunerate workers' savings and can grant loans to new investments at whatever interest rate they see fit. In this way, society benefits from the possibility of financing any type of investment that seems profitable because, however low the expected profitability of the business presented by the entrepreneur may be, it only has to be slightly greater than zero for the business to be good for the Bank.

However, the entry of new money, circulating in the economy, will cause an increase in prices. Each family now has a little more money to spend, but the entrepreneur has yet to produce new goods. The creation of money, through credit, leads society to feel the effects of inflation, which functions as a tax if it is not immediately reflected in workers' wages. But the banks feel it too. They continue to receive the same income from banking services and loans previously granted. Banks are thus dependent on entrepreneurs being successful and being able to bring more products to the market, at lower prices, and as quickly as possible. If entrepreneurs are not successful in the market, banks are forced to raise commissions and interest rates on portfolio businesses in order to guarantee their livelihood. In a full-employment society, with workers expressing great reluctance regarding possible wage losses, whenever credit deals are unsuccessful, entrepreneurs will be unable to refund the bank the capital created when the credit is granted, leaving the bank with the damage inherent to the inflation that was created in the first instance. This danger will be mitigated if entrepreneurs manage to make their businesses viable, even at the expense of several dismissals, and remain faithful in the payments of installments, interest, and commissions that the bank determines.

In 2008, professors and economists Gary Gorton and Ping He explained that bank credit cycles are an important self-contained part of business cycles. The authors showed that banking is a highly legislated economic activity. Banks operate in competition with each other. The disclosure of financial information relating to its activity occurs frequently and in great detail. In this way, when a bank knows that its competition is increasing the volume of credit granted, and doing so profitably, then it will also do so. The volume of money in circulation increases in the economy and private initiative is encouraged to create new businesses. However, when, in a short period of time, which is usually limited to one quarter, the financial indicators of bank performance retract and a given bank registers an increase in the volume of credit accompanied by lower profitability, then the remaining banks in activity adopt a position of caution and cease opening to continue granting credit. But banks continue to charge installments and interest on outstanding loans. In this situation, they withdraw money from the economy that will not be used by firms, nor by employees, in the purchase of new goods and services. Some companies are forced to go bankrupt and unemployment rises. The negative economic cycle is thus inevitable. The normal functioning of the current financial system is, itself, an automatic cause of economic crises.

Enjoying the creation of new money, banks can either participate in the capital of a new venture or, simply, indirectly stimulate the emergence of new businesses through the creation of money for consumer credit. In either case, the banks secure a share of the economy's output by creating new money.

When the bank creates money by opening a credit line for a particular branch of activity, it also finances the creation of new businesses. This is usually accompanied by the creation of new jobs. If the venture is successful, then capital and interest are returned to the bank, and the initial effects of inflation are overcome by society by obtaining more goods and services at lower prices. If the credit granted is not repaid, the bank will judicially obtain control of the firm's productive means. Therefore, whether in case of success or failure of the credit granting operation, the bank will always act as if it were a partner of the firm. And it is the creation of money for this purpose that gives it this power.

When the bank creates a line of credit to finance consumer credit, it will increase the consumer's purchasing power. The increased demand for the goods targeted by the credit line will allow companies to sell these goods at higher prices. Thus, companies' profits increase immediately through the opening of consumer credit lines. However, in the future, it is up to the worker to return capital and interest to the bank. In this case, it is in the bank's total interest that the society be able to guarantee full employment, as full compliance with the repayment of capital and interest is always ensured. Today, when society does not do this and the worker, employee, or employer, is fired or is left without a job, the bank is able to legally obtain possession of assets or income from the worker who has defaulted in order to be reimbursed for the credit it granted. Once again, banks appropriate material goods from other members of society through the simple process of creating new money.

A very similar situation happens when banks create money to finance public initiatives. Now, the banks guarantee that a significant part of society's production will revert to them in the form of taxes. But if the government guarantees a full-employment society and fails to see an effective need to collect taxes, then an important source of revenue for banks could be compromised. The fear of losing this income constitutes another foundation that, for them, seems to justify the defense of the non-implementation of full employment in our global society.

Lastly, the possibility of creating money from credit lines, which generates inflation, poses a delicate problem to banks. On the one hand, it constitutes a revenue that they do not intend to do without. On the other hand, by creating new money, banks give entrepreneurs the possibility of raising the sale price of their products across the board, making the banks' lives worse themselves. As an additional consequence, the increase in the cost of living leads all employees to demand a salary increase from their employers. If these increases are granted, then they could nullify the ability of firms to pay back principal and interest to the bank. The bank is left with a dilemma to resolve.

In 1958, professor and economist William Phillips published a study based on empirical data at the time, reporting that he found a negative relationship between inflation and unemployment and a positive relationship between employment and wages. Specifically, in the data under analysis, the author observed that unemployment decreased when inflation increased and wages increased rapidly when unemployment was low. A few years later, these statistical studies were confirmed by economists Paul Samuelson and Robert Solow. Thus, banks are justifiably afraid of the implementation of a full-employment economy in society because inflation results in a tax on them. However, in 2020 and 2021, studies carried out by several contemporary economists reveal that the relationship detected by Phillips has not been verified in most economies in the last two decades. Particularly with regard to the US economy, inflation has been under control since 1990 although economic activity and unemployment levels have fluctuated up and down over time. Inflation was controlled through the manipulation of interest rates by the central bank.

Central banks today have absolute power over society. This power comes from two sources. One is the ability to create money, which allows them to allocate purchasing power at will. The other is the possibility of increasing and reducing money in circulation, defining the rhythms of economic activity and society's well-being. At first glance, from the perspective of the first move, the creation of a full-employment society seems to endanger this power that the banks have. And the fear of losing power, in itself, is also frightening.

We have identified some of society's biggest fears. These fears condition the exercise of power. They are the ones that can lead us to lose the game since they encourage negative opportunistic behavior. Fear of losing profit, fear of losing productivity, fear of losing wages, fear of fiscal redundancy, fear of losing popularity, fear of inflation, and fear of losing power. These fears lead society to not be as productive and happy as it can be. They are what lead us to act emotionally, to play the economic game through processes of competition, and to seek to secure the largest possible share of society's total income in the first instance. We rush into actions such as strikes and protests, bribes and influence peddling, or wars and blackmail, always with the aim of taking immediate advantage for ourselves, but detrimentally to another fraction of society. However, as the society of lions has shown us, the fear of loss gets in the way, and the strength of power is not measured by the ability to demand. The strength of power is measured by the ability to do.

Mate in 7

In society, as in chess, decisions between the two players alternate, and positive opportunistic behavior is followed by the possibility of negative opportunistic behavior. To win the game, society must know, in its deepest depths, that it can trust itself. To win the game, society has to ensure that the last move is made by positive opportunistic behavior, making checkmate.

When we allow fear to rule our decision-making process, we define rules for controlling individual behavior based on the penalty. The elaboration of this type of rule is intended to face an immediate objective of preventing people from acting in a certain way or, alternatively, to make them obey the instruction received, regardless of their will. In chess, it is the equivalent of a move that is not thought through and whose consequences only appear to be an immediate benefit. Thus, "blunders, errors, and inaccuracies" frequently appear.

When we are focused on playing the best possible game, we go deeper into the analysis of the possible consequences of our plays. We reflect before acting. We often come to the conclusion that we can, and must, sacrifice our Queen to win the game. We fully master our fear of loss. We discover the "brilliant" plays and make sure they are followed by "great and good" ones. We trust ourselves.

A stunning example of how difficult it is to make the right decisions when trying to channel the behavior of other members of society in a positive direction was given by a father when faced with his son's actions. On a busy afternoon, in the middle of a shopping center, after a four-year-old boy threw himself to the ground, screaming, kicking, and throwing a huge and embarrassing tantrum, the father reacted by imitating the little one! He did exactly the same! When the child saw his father on the floor, screaming and moving as he was doing, simply stopped his tantrum, and stared at him in amazement.

The example set by this father is absolutely wonderful. This man told his son that, to him, he is the most important person on the Earth, regardless of everything else around them. This man also told his son that he can act however he wants, but his father is also free to react as he sees fit. And both will be acting before the rest of society. Psychology explains that the probable reason why the child stopped his outburst of anger was that he mentally moved away from the initial emotional reaction to adopt a rational process where doubt settled in his mind: "What a strange thing is that my father is doing! Why is my father behaving this way?"

This example provides a strong foundation for how to build a society where we can trust each other. First, at all times, the father's behavior was oriented toward the positive mode. The father was not afraid of ridicule. The father tried to find the best solution for his son to reflect on what he was doing, without being guided by fear. The father did not seek to demand obedience. The father acted with a focus on the future. The father believed that the son would learn from his reaction and give the best answer. The father understood that the best way to control his son's tantrums would be through reason. The father tried to make the child realize that it is he who has to decide to "behave well" instead of his father forcing him to do so. From now on, the father seeks to build a solid foundation of trust in his son. He tries that, in the future, the son can reason about his emotional impulses before acting.

In this case, the negative opportunistic behavior of the child was followed by the positive opportunistic behavior of the father. Creating the conditions for positive opportunistic behavior to dominate our society is not an intuitive process. It is the implementation of a reward-based system, which, through successive plays, renders ineffective any desire to adopt negative opportunistic behaviors.

Winning the game

Whatever the opening move, from the outset, it will condition the possible responses on the part of the opponent. By itself, the opening move is never decisive. To win the game, the opening is important, but the position of the pieces has to be well consolidated with the following moves.

#1 Enacting full-employment

In chess, the first move is intended to achieve three goals simultaneously: to start the development of our pieces; initiate control of the center of the board; and avoid losing valuable pieces. The opening is crucial because the players' first moves dictate the pace the match will take.

To maximize productivity, society's first choice is to secure private property. Economics has already shown that the increase in processes of expropriation as the result of labor effort leads to a decrease in productivity. Society has also realized that it is through increased production of the most diverse goods and services that the well-being of all is guaranteed through exchange processes. Therefore, the granting of private property is an incentive for entrepreneurship and is crucial to ensure the well-being of all.

However, the entrepreneur becomes even more productive when, at the same time, he is able to resort to the additional work of other people, while enjoying an ever-growing market to place all his production. The positive effects of economies of scale, for the vast majority of economic activities, are widely recognized. Entrepreneurs realized a long time ago that the price at which they can sell their products will be better the greater the demand for them. It is therefore in the interest of every monopolist that his potential customers be in large numbers, and that everyone has a job. It is in this circumstance that the monopolist is able to maximize an ever-increasing profit.

The combination of the protection of private property with the existence of full employment provides the optimal conditions for maximizing society's productivity. First, society creates conditions to minimize less productive work, performed in tired conditions. Second, society no longer needs to redistribute income from those who work to those who do not, as happens in the fiscal process of expropriation to which we are all subject today. Maximizing society's productivity requires a situation of full employment.

Enacting full employment in society will exacerbate the impetus of our greatest adversaries, which are our fears and negative opportunistic behaviors. In chess, many times, our fears are faced with the sacrifice of the Queen. But, sacrificing our Queen is a decision that is only possible when we know in advance how we are going to play next. In order to control the many fears triggered by the idea of enacting a full-employment society, and be aware that this is the way to win the game, we have to understand in advance which movements we are going to execute after this step is concluded.

One of the first fears that arise with the decree of a full-employment society is the fear of "laziness". We all know that there are good and bad workers. We also know that people act in a certain way because they want to, and because they can. Bad workers are only bad because they want to, and because they can. And it is with this current condition of a person being able to perform a function for which he has no talent or vocation, that society has to learn to deal with.

Another fear that arises in society in the face of the possibility of enacting full employment concerns the irregularity of aggregate demand directed at firms' products. In 1992, the economists Christopher Carroll, Robert Hall, and Stephen Zeldes demonstrated that the consumer adjusts his consumption patterns depending on the uncertainty of his future income and his preference for consuming in the present. This behavior results in an irregularity in the demand for the products produced by firms, which occurs over time, and it is one that entrepreneurs cannot control. Consequently, if the economy operates under a regime of free competition and an open market, then firms will have to go through times when there is a need to reduce wages, fire people, or resort to both solutions.

The perception, on the part of entrepreneurs, of the combination between the heterogeneity of the workforce and the potential irregularity of the demand that is directed toward the firm's products, makes employers have a very effective need to adjust the wages they pay and the number of employees they employ. And this faculty must be guaranteed to them. Therefore, with the safeguard of the full-employment society, it is necessary that people who are going to be fired from a company, where they are being unproductive, are immediately integrated into another company, where they are needed.

Ensuring general freedom to fire, being a faculty that all firms must hold, stirs up the greatest fear of all workers: being unable to safeguard a source of stable income that allows them to face the future with peace of mind. However, when the full-employment society is enacted, all people see their need for survival guaranteed. The fact that an individual is fired from a firm does not affect his future, as he will immediately be integrated into another company where he is being more precise. Thus, what is truly at stake is not the survival of each human being, but rather the quality of life that each person manages to get from their working condition.

The fact that society grants the employer the right to dismiss at will implies imposing on the worker the acceptance of the risk of not knowing in which firm the person might end up. And here comes another fear that society has to learn to deal with. Worker or employer, every human being likes to feel that he has conditions to work in the place he wants, with the people he wants.

To overcome these multiple fears, it is necessary for society to decide to play the economic game positively, in a cooperative manner. Thus, we can create operating rules that make society reliable. This requires the creation of rules that encourage positive opportunistic behavior, both from employees and employers, and that are accepted by all, from the very beginning.

On the employer's side, there is a need to lower wages or lay off employees in two different circumstances: 1) when the demand for its product decreases and the company finds that it is overstaffed; and 2) when faced with a worker without a personal profile to perform that function. In the first case, the worker will be dismissed from the company, due to the termination of his job, and will join another company, hopefully, maintaining his current remuneration. In the second case, so that the negative opportunistic behavior is continuously inhibited and the positive opportunistic behavior is encouraged, the worker will enter the second company with a lower salary "x %" in relation to his current one. Salary is the worker's reward and the decrease in reward acts as an inhibitor of possible negative opportunistic behavior on the part of the worker who decides to adopt a "lazy" attitude.

On the worker's side, the implementation of a full-employment society gives the employee greater power to change employer whenever he sees fit. It is intended that a person be free to resign whenever being mistreated by their employer. If so, the employer who mistreats his employees ends up having to pay more to have someone working for him or, sooner or later, reverses his way of acting toward employees. Providing the worker with the ability to say goodbye whenever he wants, without fear of having a loss of income, results in a direct incentive for the development of positive opportunistic behavior on the part of the employer.

The implementation of a full-employment society cannot be successful if it is not accompanied by the freedom of employers, and employees, to fire and resign, respectively. At the same time, both must be free to carry out salary renegotiations whenever they see fit. With these measures, society takes firm steps toward becoming free, reliable, and respectful.

To be successful, society has to create an organization

that allows it to carry out the relocation of people in an expeditious and functional way. And this is not an easy task. On the one hand, it is necessary to agree on a set of rules, unanimously accepted by the people, that will allow the relocation of workers. On the other hand, in light of the wage loss rule of "x %" for the bad employee who is dismissed, it is necessary to create a database that allows society to check these values. In order for these goals to be achieved, it is necessary to create "Employment Centers" where employees and employers can go to announce their needs. But it is also necessary to resort to the intelligent use of software.

With this institutional framework, both the employer and the employee are better off. The employer becomes aware that he can be as productive as possible, given the existing technology, and becomes even more efficient in managing his business units. The employee, in turn, is encouraged to perform the function for which he has the most vocation and talent, instead of simply looking for a "pot", which just enables him to have a stable income and which simply allows him to consume what he wants without having to pay concerns about the contribution it makes to the rest of the community. For the employee, having a well-paid job where performance is mediocre can no longer be a consistent situation over time. And the person quickly becomes aware of that fact. In addition, the same person is calmer because the comfort of their day-to-day life no longer depends on having to hold that place, doing things that they do not even like to do. The full-employment society that adopts this type of rule calms some of its members' fears: the fear of loss of productivity and the fear of loss of wages.

As in chess, it is through the analysis of the successive consequences of the adoption of a given step that we are previously able to figure out the best sequence of moves. And this analysis has not yet been properly deepened. From what has been exposed above, there are some additional problems to which the full-employment society still does not respond. They are: 1) how are people who have just lost their jobs be replaced?; 2) since society has to employ all people without work, how is the survival of employers safeguarded?; 3) after adopting the full-employment society, with firms' profits tending to zero, how will society proceed with the creation of new firms if the investment is compromised due to the lack of profits that can finance it?; and 4) given that it is up to employers to decide the selling price of their products, and they have just been granted the power to freely dismiss and renegotiate the remuneration of employees, what guarantees do workers have that their living conditions do not worsen when the society decrees the situation of full employment?

Once again, fear can trigger negative opportunistic behaviors in opposition to the creation of a full-employment society. Similar to what is required of the society of lions to improve their quality of life, we too need to analyze the situation before making hasty decisions based on fear. The creation of reliable and unanimously accepted rules by society, upon which we can all freely evolve, requires the recognition of the general public that the legislator is focused on stimulating positive opportunistic behavior and inhibiting negative opportunistic behavior. In this context, each of the four doubts raised in the previous paragraph is pertinent to the analysis of the possibility of creating a full-employment society.

Achieving unanimous acceptance of criteria for the relocation of people who have lost their jobs is a difficult task for the legislator. First, employees will want to be the ones to choose where they want to go. And second, employers, in order to ensure good management of their business, want to keep wage expenses at the same level they were before having more employees joining their firms. Thus, the legislator must seek to respond to these two needs, while remaining focused on promoting positive opportunistic behavior.

From the worker's point of view, when we enact a full-employment society, he knows that he can say goodbye, go to the "Employment Center" and start working immediately at another company. At the same time, the worker also knows that he can first look for another company and only say goodbye when this new agreement is signed. In the first situation, it is the "Employment Center" that best knows which firms are most in need of a person with the qualifications of each worker. So, it makes sense for the "Employment Center" to place the person. In the second case, it is the worker himself who already has the ability to seek work for the company that seems most attractive to him, without having to resort to third-party support. It is concluded that the worker does not really need to worry about the firm where the "Employment Center" will place him, since society endows him with the power to continue looking for his place in case a choice is, eventually, inappropriate. Workers and society become aware that each individual will be, more and more, "the right person, in the right place, at the right time."

The first question is thus solved.

In a full-employment society, the survival of employers can be questioned and requires a pertinent analysis. Given that society will live in full employment then, every time a person wants to create a new firm, the employer will be forced to remove employees from existing companies. To attract these people, the employer will have to increase their remuneration. Employers will thus be fully aware that their profit decreases. Additionally, every company, with a business going on, will find that, in order to keep good employees, it will have to pay them a higher salary to dissuade the competition's harassment of its good workers. Thus, with the implementation of the full-employment society, employers know that there will be a reduction in profit at the expense of a general increase in wages.

But, contrary wise to what intuitive thinking dictates, profit is not an essential requirement for the existence of firms. Just as a bishop, a knight, or a rook are crucial pieces for the harmonious development of our moves on the chessboard, firms are also fundamental pieces in the harmonious development of society. But it is necessary to recognize that firms are made up of employers and employees and that everyone knows, and accepts, their rules for moving around the chessboard. At the limit, we find the sole proprietorship with a single worker, in which the worker is just an employee who works for himself. In any case, whether when the company is made up of just one person, or when the company is made up of hundreds or thousands of people, the contribution that each firm makes to society is always confined to the set of goods and services it provides to others. If firms did not exist, society would not be able to have an enormous diversity of goods and services at its disposal. But profit is not essential for this to happen.

Profit is simply the difference between the selling price of goods and services produced by firms and their cost of production. This production cost involves all operational, extraordinary, financial, and tax costs that were necessary to make that production possible. Operating costs include all costs with merchandise, raw materials, external supplies, and services, research and development expenses, amortization of fixed assets, and personnel costs. Finally, personnel costs include the employer's remuneration and the remuneration of employees. Thus, the entrepreneur's salary is not at stake when the full-employment society is decreed and his survival is, of course, guaranteed.

The second doubt is clarified.

But the third question raises doubts about society's ability to engage in new ventures under a zero-profit reality which is induced by an institutional environment of full employment. This issue still needs special attention.

In today's economies, but more so in underdeveloped and developing ones, people are often dedicated to creating their own jobs. The opening of small-capacity business units necessarily inhibits the productivity that these companies are able to achieve. In 2019, the OECD (Organization for Economic Co-operation and Development) published a report on entrepreneurship prospects for SMEs (Small and Medium Enterprises) in its 38 member countries, which bring together the most advanced economies in the world. The report states that two out of three people work for an SME. This report also points out that, in these 38 most developed economies in the world, and in the period between 2002 and 2017, the vast majority of new job creation took place in sectors with below-average productivity. The report also underlines that SMEs are leading the growth in the number of jobs in OECD countries, but they need greater investments in terms of the qualifications of their workers, innovation, and technology in order to reach higher levels of productivity. In the present institutional environment, of our global society, it is concluded that the levels of productivity and well-being that we have managed to achieve already fall short of what is possible to obtain due to a lack of appropriate funding.

The fourth question, in turn, casts doubt on the safety of workers who consider that their level of well-being is exposed to the feelings of the owners of the productive means due to the fact that they control, simultaneously, the value of wages paid, the amounts of goods and services offered for sale, and the respective selling price of its products. However, once full employment is decreed, with the conditions listed above, there will be freedom for wage renegotiation in conjunction with the fact that the sale price of products is always limited by the maximum value that the consumer is willing to pay for them, given its budget allocation. As a result, entrepreneurs begin to act in accordance with the positive dynamics of the market. First, the wages of all workers will have significant upward pressure. Second, the selling price of products will have a greater downward trend. This tendency will be all the more accentuated the greater the freedom that the economy is granting its members to create new firms and operate them in a regime of free competition. Both the first and second situations require a deeper analysis.

In the first case, workers' fears can be alleviated if society unanimously accepts a priority for relocating people to the most profitable firms, with the highest average salary, or where there are the greatest salary inequalities among workers. Whenever companies show exaggerated profits, based on negative opportunistic behavior close to a monopoly situation, society introduces a stimulus to their moderation through the preferential placement of unemployed people in these companies. In this case, we can have two negative emotional reactions from the owners of these companies and their employees. In the first step, the total amount earmarked for wages in the very profitable firm's budget can be divided by the new number of workers. In this assumption, all workers are initially dissatisfied with the fact that they are earning less. In the second phase, the negative reaction on the part of the firm's owners is now due to the fact that they realize that they really have to increase the salaries paid, at least to guarantee the permanence of the best employees, which always results in the benefit of the good workers of the firm. The adoption of a priority of placing workers in the most profitable companies, by itself, constitutes a stimulus for the increase of the wages of the workers. Thus, the initial, instinctive, and emotional reaction of the firm's workers is not justified.

The priority placement of unemployed workers in companies with the highest average salary leads to people being placed first in the most productive sectors of the economy. The placement of unemployed people in companies that show greater wage inequalities will also constitute a stimulus for these inequalities to be mitigated. In 2023, in Portugal, the weekly newspaper "Expresso" reported that the salary of the Executive Director of the distribution company "Jerónimo Martins" was about 186 times higher than the average gross salary of the company's other employees. But the same newspaper also stressed that this is not an isolated case. Specifically, the Executive Director of "Sonae", another large distribution company, receives 82 times more than the average employee, and, on average, the Executive Directors of companies in the PSI index (Portuguese Stock Index), which aggregates the largest companies listed on Euronext Lisbon, earn 36 times more than the remaining workers. As economics has shown, the worker's productivity decreases more and more, the greater the part of his production that is expropriated. It is concluded that the acceptance of these rules, by society, constitutes a strong stimulus for the adoption of positive opportunistic behaviors, and inhibition of negative opportunistic behaviors, which benefits everyone.

Finally, it should be noted that the efficiency of the full-employment society increases when people are more aware of which economic activities are better remunerated. Today, in Portugal, there is a shortage of welders, plumbers, electricians, carpenters, refrigeration technicians, and many other professions of a more manual and, allegedly, less intellectual nature. This situation is a consequence of a reversal of society's focus. In the first two-thirds of the 20th century, Portuguese society lived in an environment of low productivity, greatly conditioned by the absence of effective educational and training processes. At that time, most individuals learned a profession from older people, and most workers were dedicated to manual professions. The average earnings of each person were low because society's output was low and was shared by the entire population. People with higher education were few and this situation led to them charging a lot for their services. With the creation of conditions that allowed a greater number of people to acquire higher academic training, all parents in general, guided by the desire to provide their children with the best possible living conditions, began to pressure young people to continue their academic studies while losing the notion about the value that other professional activities, of a more manual nature, have for society. Today, in Portugal, a welder, a refrigeration technician, or a heavy-duty car driver, all earn a monthly salary higher than most people who have taken a university course. But society has lost this notion due to a lack of adequate and timely disclosure of relevant information.

Nonetheless, the concerns raised by the third and fourth questions are still not perfectly controlled because entrepreneurs remain fearful with regard to their future investment capacity and workers are not yet completely calm about the purchase price they will have to pay for the products they need to live. So that society can adequately respond to the fears that were raised there, these two questions refer us to the analysis of the financial system.

Before moving on to the next move, we can thus summarize the basic conditions necessary to implement the full-employment society: 1) guaranteeing employment to all people who request it; 2) giving total freedom for the renegotiation of wages, working hours and working conditions, between employers and employees; 3) placing workers in companies or activity sectors that have higher profits; 4) placing workers in companies and sectors of activity that have greater wage inequality; 5) placing workers in companies and activity sectors that have a higher average salary; and 6) making effective dissemination of this data so that the educational efforts of parents, and training of society in general, are directed to where they are most needed.

Society becomes more reliable after full employment is enacted based on the rules identified above. The homeless cease to exist and society can finally take care of itself. The full-employment society entails a set of advantages that only our bounded rationality prevents us from readily putting them into practice. But the doubts regarding society's capacity to generate new investments, and the workers' fears regarding the possibility of worsening social inequalities, with a decrease in their living conditions, have yet to be duly clarified. In chess, the player consolidates his position through a series of successive moves. Here, the weakness that is reflected by society's exposure to these fears also requires the adoption of institutional rules, unanimously accepted, and that will work as additional moves in our game. These institutional rules, which are necessary, extend beyond the implementation of the full-employment society.

#2 Preventing the use of collateral in the granting of credit

In the game of chess, the second move is one of the most interesting to analyze. The first objective of the second move is to continue to develop the positioning of our pieces on the board, according to the impetus that the first move provided. However, this second move may be conditioned by the opening move that our antagonist chose to make. The second move thus assumes greater complexity, which comes from the need to identify the consequences resulting from our first move, as well as the reaction of our opponent.

In this last case, the opponent's reaction poses difficulties for us. Doubts regarding society's capacity to generate new investments and workers' fears regarding the possibility of worsening social inequalities and worsening of their living conditions, are both still to be duly clarified. However, one of the functions of the financial system is precisely to meet the firms' financing needs. It is therefore important to understand the current functioning of the financial system before realizing which rules can be unanimously accepted by society and that stimulate positive opportunistic behavior by all its members.

Bank revenues come from two sources: the provision of services, and interest. The provision of banking services can be summarized into two types: provision of means of payment and custody of valuables. Banks provide customers with checks, ATM cards to be used in Automated Teller Machines, services for transferring funds between customer accounts, and other related services, facilitating the completion of commercial transactions in the economy. Additionally, banks provide safekeeping services, allowing people to trust their banks to retain part of their savings or belongings, knowing that, there, those goods are not damaged or lost. These revenues are usually called commissions. In turn, revenues inherent to credit operations are commonly known as interest. Although banks create money to extend credit to their customers, the money thus created is not accounted for as bank income. In the first phase, the money is given to the customer through the granting of consumer or investment credit. Thus, the money created by the financial system enters into circulation in the real economy by the hand of the debtor. When entering the economy, this additional money will create inflation. Since people have more money at their disposal and will buy the products that are already produced, the prices of different goods and services rise across the economy. This inflation is also felt by the bank. When the customer returns the principal and interest, the principal is treated as if it were a refund.

Despite the appearance that commercial banks get hold of the outcome of the work of the remaining society members, the truth is that central banks are the ones who control the creation of money. In 2021, in Portugal, the annual report of the accounts of "Banco Montepio," which is a commercial bank, reveals that, in this period and in average terms, credit granted to customers decreased by around 122 million euros, while resources coming from central banks increased by more than 1 billion euros. "Banco Montepio" increased its funds with a view to future credit operations. This means that the income inherent to the interest that banks charge on credit operations is, in most cases, simply an intermediation commission that corresponds to the difference between the interest they charge on credit operations to their customers and the interest they pay, both to central banks, for the funds made available, and to their customers' savings, for portfolio deposits. This intermediation commission is usually called the financial margin.

The functioning of the financial system is quite simple and acceptable when central banks are owned by the state and operate under the purview of the government. However, there are countries in the world where the central bank is privately owned and managed autonomously. Both central banks and commercial banks play a decisive role in society by providing the necessary financing so that firms and individuals can acquire the most diverse products and services. But the action of these financial system entities is also conditioned by the fears they have regarding negative opportunistic behavior on the part of the private sector of the economy.

As the financial system recognizes that there is an asymmetry in the available information between the true financial strength of the potential debtor of a credit operation and that which is perceived by the bank, then banks fear that reality is worse than perception and, therefore, tend to condition the carrying out of credit operations to the provision of collateral by their customers. Banks seek to protect themselves from the bad faith of businessmen and consumers, or from their own incompetence in assessing their customers' financial situation, ensuring a penalty mechanism for the debtor in the event of non-compliance. Guided by fear, banks seek to protect themselves from the negative opportunistic behavior of other members of society.

When a credit is granted, two things can happen: 1) either it is successful, or 2) the customer is unable to repay the bank in accordance with the agreed plan. When credit is successful, resorting to the use of real guarantees has harmful effects on society. In this case, and ultimately, the use of a real guarantee proved to be perfectly unnecessary since the customer, based on the normal development of his economic activity, complied with what was contracted in the credit operation. But, in the first instance, the banks conditioned the attribution of credit only to customers who possess goods to protect credit operations. This results in an important social inequality that prevents people, who are not previously owners of any relevant material asset, from being able to benefit from the support of the financial system, even if they are competent in what they do or have good business ideas. All of society loses out because many companies are not born to increase the quantity of goods and services available to everyone at lower prices. On the other hand, when credit is unsuccessful, recourse to normal legal mechanisms should be sufficient for the bank to be compensated for its loss. When there is an effective judicial system there is no need to resort to the use of real guarantees in the first instance. The use of real guarantees for granting credit inhibits society from being more productive.

However, there is another loss to society. The use of collateral in the granting of credit also induces banks not to facilitate the eventual renegotiation of loans in progress, even if the firms' businesses are still viable. In these cases, banks often chose to foreclose on collateral instead of keeping firms in business. This is a situation of negative opportunistic behavior since the bank itself will be living worse off the greater the number of other banks acting in the same way.

Despite the above-identified problems, the financial system plays a very important role in the prior assessment of the good, or bad, prospects for success that investment projects exhibit. Often, by saying "no" to a loan application, the bank is helping society to avoid wasting resources on that specific undertaking. By saying "no" to a credit request, the bank is preventing the proliferation of inflation. But this decision must be based solely on the assessment that the bank makes of the business potential that is presented to it and cannot be previously conditioned by the existence of goods that can be given, in the guarantee of the fulfillment of the agreement with the bank, by the debtor.

Interestingly, if society implements the situation of full employment, the financial system's legitimate fears regarding debtors' repayment capacity are completely quelled. First, the bank is absolutely certain that the debtor will always have, in the future, the financial means to reimburse the sums received. Second, banks can completely dispense with any type of real guarantee, enabling a greater number of credit operations than those they approve right now.

These stimuli to positive opportunistic behavior come to calm part of the doubts regarding society's ability to make new investments and ensure the maintenance of workers' living conditions. However, in a full-employment society, banks too can fire all employees they consider surplus. Also, banks are free to charge their customers as high as possible for the services they render to society. With regard to the relocation of employees and motivation of employers, the rules defined in the first move guarantee that there is a tendency to encourage balance in the exercise of economic activity and respect for all people. However, corporate profits continue to tend toward zero and workers are not sure of having access to credit when they will intend to create new companies. The abolition of the use of collateral is a necessary step for the financial system to make a greater contribution to raising the levels of well-being in society. It is a measure that consolidates the implementation of the full-employment society, signaling to the population that there is a collective effort in the sense of raising the levels of well-being of all, without exception. But the abolition of the use of real guarantees in credit operations is not enough to guarantee that economic activity does not foster social inequality or that the living conditions of the entire population are assured.

#3 Preventing the creation of money for consumer credit

In chess, it is unanimously accepted that the strength of a knight on the chessboard is measured by the number of squares it manages to touch. When in starting position, the knight only controls 4 squares of the play space. But after the first move, if the knight jumps to the center, it now controls 9 squares, out of the 64 on the board. The horse in the center is very strong. The horse acquires greater preponderance when it controls an important part of the development of the opponent's game.

Economics explains that an important factor in safeguarding the well-being of the population lies in society's ability to control inflation. We easily perceive that the creation of money for granting credit to citizens is a way of immediately providing purchasing power to people who will restore this purchasing capacity in the future. However, the granting of credit can come from two sources: 1) either it comes from customers' savings deposited in credit institutions; 2) or it may originate from lines of credit made available by central banks to commercial banks.

When we are dealing with the granting of consumer credit, and the operation comes from customers' savings deposited in the bank, then we are facing a situation in which there is a temporary exchange between two consumers. Using the bank as an intermediary, the depositor client lends his savings, in the present, to a person who now needs that purchasing power and is willing to return that amount in the future. The bank simply provides an intermediary service for which it charges a fee. This operation does not generate inflation because one individual's consumption corresponds to another's savings, and this situation will be symmetrical in the future. The money available in circulation in society never changes.

When the granting of consumer credit comes from the creation of new money, there is an increase in money in circulation throughout the economy. This situation causes a general increase in prices and makes "almost all" members of society's life worse. "Almost all" because employers get better. The increase in the amount of money in circulation will mean that, immediately, firms can increase their selling prices, while all consumers will have to pay a higher price to acquire the goods and services they need. Given that wages do not immediately adjust upward, and the firms' products are already produced, the creation of new money to be used in the granting of consumer credit encourages a transfer of money from workers' wages to firms that, in this way, increase their profits. Currently, social inequality is based on the creation of money for the granting of consumer credit.

The increase in the perception of the existence of social inequalities between employees and employers has the same result as the expropriation of part of the worker's production. And economics has already shown that productivity decreases when this happens. Consequently, despite society's limited awareness of this fact, creating money to grant consumer credit is negative opportunistic behavior. Each bank gets worse off the greater the number of banks resorting to the creation of new money to grant consumer credit.

The possibility of creating new money for granting consumer credit also means that commercial banks do not need to remunerate customer savings above the amount at which central banks make lines of credit available to them. Thus, if central banks create money out of thin air and lend money to commercial banks at zero cost, being satisfied with the return of the capital, commercial banks also do not need to pay anything to their customers for their deposited savings in banking institutions. Consequently, abolishing the possibility of creating new money for the concession of consumer credit brings yet another benefit to workers: they immediately ensure a higher return on their savings.

It is, therefore, concluded that this step allows society to acquire greater control over the levels of inflation and distribution of purchasing power that its citizens have to deal with. But the two doubts raised above, regarding the guarantee of living conditions for the entire population and the capacity of firms to make new ventures, although more tenuous, still keep a dangerous small flame burning.

#4 Ensuring that money creation is earmarked for the granting of investment credit

The bishop is a very important piece in the game of chess. It is a piece that moves diagonally. At the start of the game, each player has a bishop on the white square and a bishop on the black square. From its square, each bishop can be moved to any free square that is located in a corridor, diagonal to its position, formed by the squares of its color. It has some characteristics that are particularly distinctive from other pieces in the chess game. This difference concerns the increase in its value as the game time passes. First, given that the bishop controls the largest number of squares due to the free space on the board, the value of the bishop on the white squares will differ from the value of the bishop on the black squares, being more valuable the one that faces fewer pawns occupying the squares of its color. That is, the white bishop has more value the smaller the number of pawns located on white squares on the board. Indeed, as the game evolves and fewer and fewer pieces are left on the board, the bishops acquire added value due to the fact that they are able to control an ever-increasing space. When the board is empty, a bishop placed in the center controls a total of 15 squares, out of the 64 that the chess board has.

In economics, and similar to what happens in the game of chess, society's ability to use money is also a very important piece to guarantee the well-being of populations. Likewise, as economic activity develops, society's capacity to create more money also allows it to stimulate positive opportunistic behavior by economic agents. Banks stimulate a particular sector of economic activity when they create lines of credit dedicated to that sector. If credit is aimed at the consumer, then producers feel the increase of the aggregate demand directed toward them. And this allows firms to increase the selling price of their products, increasing their profits. If the market is free, increased profits will stimulate increased investment in the market, which in turn fosters increased competition and leads to more goods available to society at lower prices. On the other hand, if credit is aimed at investors, then banks will increase new investments by firms in that sector of economic activity. This results in increased competition in the market, which will result in an increase in available goods at lower prices. At first, whether through consumer credit or through investment credit, people's positive opportunistic behavior is stimulated when banks create money. All people live better the greater the number of actions of this nature that occur in society.

However, in a second moment, under the current rules of the financial system's operation, the money created by the banks has to be returned, plus interest. Therefore, in this second moment, the banks will withdraw money from the economy. Now, in response to the diminishing purchasing power of aggregate demand, producers are forced to reduce their production, reduce their staff, reduce wages paid, raise selling prices, or combine all these measures to maintain the same profit margins. The whole society is forced to live worse. If the credit is initially intended for consumption, this money is withdrawn from consumers. In the initial phase, producers are the ones who profit the most from the practice of creating new money for the concession of consumer credit. In the final stage, consumers are the ones who pay. Society exacerbates social inequalities by creating money dedicated to consumer credit. On the other hand, when the money created by the banks is dedicated to firms' investment, it is the producers who will return to the bank the capital they received in the first moment, plus interest. But this return concerns the profits obtained from the sale of products that were successful in the market. No harmful action results for society when the credit granted to the investment is successful, nor does it result in any stimulus to the negative opportunistic behavior of anyone.

We thus have two desirable situations: 1) that the creation of money is devoted exclusively to the granting of credit for investment; and 2) that this investment is successful. However, if investment credit is granted for the development of a ruinous business, which is not accepted by the market, then, in the future, banks will demand the return of an amount of capital and interest that the entrepreneur does not have how to comply with. Consequently, the entrepreneur is forced to reduce his usual consumption pattern in order to be able to return whatever it is to the bank. In this context, the aggregate demand directed at all companies decreases, and society is provided with a stimulus for generalized negative opportunistic behavior. It is, therefore, concluded that the success of investments made by entrepreneurs is absolutely essential for the creation of money by banks to be virtuous for society.

We realize today that the importance of controlling how money is created in society is similar to the importance of bishops in winning the game of chess. As time goes by, only the creation of money for lending to investment projects can be consistently virtuous for society. The importance of creating money to raise society's levels of well-being directly depends on the ability of entrepreneurs to create value for all through the development of new businesses. Only then can society effectively, and consistently, control the stimulus for positive opportunistic behavior by all people.

Commercial banking reaps immense benefits from the adoption of this measure by the financial system. But, this conclusion is not intuitive. At first glance, it appears that society is limiting banks' current freedom to create money as they see fit. Intuitively, this situation suggests a worsening situation for the banks, as it seems that they are no longer able to take advantage of profit opportunities in consumer credit operations. But a more rational analysis allows us to conclude that consumer credit operations are not inhibited. They are only limited to being carried out by banks using people's savings. Furthermore, the creation of new money by banks is always an inflation-generating act. Inflation works as a tax for society as a whole, but it is a tax that is always felt more by the banks in relation to the rest of the population because the money created at moment zero serves to provide purchasing power to producers or consumers, but not to the bank. While the former can already increase their investment or consumption power by receiving an increase in their purchasing power through the credit granted to them, banks, for their part, only improve their situation later on, when the capital and interest are returned to them by creditors. By defining the exclusivity of creating money for granting investment credit, banks will ensure that they live consistently better.

When we combine the abolition of the use of collateral in credit operations, with the impediment to the creation of new money to finance consumption, while guaranteeing the possibility of creating money exclusively to finance investment credit operations, we reach an extremely advantageous situation for commercial banking, but which also underlines the tremendous importance of central banks' role for society to ensure economic prosperity. Once again, this is not an intuitive situation, both for ordinary citizens and for the banks involved in the financial system.

Specifically, the current functioning of the financial

system defines an extremely tight regulatory system, which commercial banking has to comply with due to the guidelines issued by central banks. These guidelines, in the aspects that directly impact the granting of credit, respect the credit limits that banks are authorized to grant, respect the level of real guarantees that the granting of these credits must exhibit, and respect the cost that the money just created by central banks has for commercial banks. When central banks allocate lines of credit to commercial banks, they are obliged to return to the central bank the new money that has just been created, plus the interest that the central bank defines. Before the central bank, the commercial bank is, in every way, similar to an entrepreneur who needs to be successful in his business to be able to return to his creditor the purchasing power attributed to him through the granting of credit. In this context, commercial banks owe obedience to central banks.

Commercial banks are important providers of financial intermediation services that operate at two different levels. There is a level of intervention through which commercial banking performs intertemporal financial intermediation, lending, in the present, people's savings, which will be returned to their depositors in the future. In this case, the bank retains an intermediation commission for providing the service it provides to society. There is another level of intervention in which the commercial bank lends, in the present, the money created by the central bank and which it will have to return in the future, plus interest. In this context, commercial banking is, once again, providing a financial intermediation service, which, in this case, happens to be between the money created by the central bank and the debtor. Consequently, if commercial banking intervenes in financial activity only as an effective intermediary between the parties involved, the financial system can reach levels of efficiency as high as the competence of central banks in deciding on credit operations. As long as the creation of new money is confined to the central bank and the commercial bank acts only as an intermediary and not as a debtor, then, in a full-employment economy, no commercial bank is in real danger of failure.

In addition to financial intermediation activity with the central bank, currently, commercial banking also creates new money by granting credit from a proportion of the customer deposits it has in its portfolio. If the commercial bank is only authorized by the central bank to create money for the granting of investment credit, then we verify that the commercial bank only runs the effective risk of bankruptcy when the investment project that benefited from the credit operation is unsuccessful.

The central bank has only two responsibilities: 1) to control the inflation levels of the economy by controlling the creation of new money, and 2) to ensure the credibility of the financial system. If the financial system combines the three measures – the abolition of the use of collateral in credit operations, the impediment to the creation of new money to finance consumption, and the reserve of the ability to create money solely to finance investment credit operations – then the central bank acquires conditions to guarantee that the control of inflation levels does not depend on the use of the interest rate for that purpose. In other words, and contrary to what happens today, society will be sure that the financial system will stimulate positive opportunistic behavior.

Of the many contributions that Economics has made to make economic and social development a reality, the many studies focused on measures to control inflation and its effects on populations stand out. In 2019, professors and economists Fernando Alvarez, Martín Beraja, Martín Gonzalez-Rozada, and Pablo Andrés Neumeyer showed that the frequency of price increases and decreases is similar when inflation levels are low. That is, economics has shown that inflation levels only stimulate human negative opportunistic behavior when inflation exceeds a given threshold. The authors focused their study on empirical data provided by the economies of Argentina, the Eurozone, Poland, Mexico, Brazil, the United States, Israel, and Norway. They concluded that, in general, the negative effects of inflation only begin to be felt when it exceeds 5% per year.

Today, society knows that the creation of money by banks is beneficial to economic development whenever it is dedicated to the granting of investment credit while the investments are successful. We also know that banks encourage negative opportunistic behavior by economic agents whenever they withdraw money from the economy. Additionally, during the entire period of time that a company is a creditor of the financial system, the bank is a partner of the investor, since it also holds part of the capital that finances the company's assets. Then, the central bank can allow the financial system to create money at will for lending to investment as long as inflation levels remain below a given threshold value. The central bank can also prevent money creation when this level of inflation is threatened.

Cumulatively, the financial system can guarantee that the bank does not withdraw money from the economy if the participation in the firm's capital acquires a more lasting character. When banks participate in the capital of firms as creditors, they are remunerated with capital and interest during the term of the loan. If this participation acquires a relatively unlimited character in time, the bank starts to sign an initial agreement, at the time of granting credit, which is focused on the quality of the firm's business and never on the objective of appropriating collateral. The bank's permanence in the firm's capital will constitute an important source of remuneration for the bank that will remain over time. Banks become partners with firms for a longer period. In this context, bank failure is no longer possible. On the one hand, the commercial bank acts only as a financial intermediary. Therefore, each bank is an important service provider that can be replaced by another without any negative consequences for society. On the other hand, the bankruptcy of firms will never entail the loss of savings for any citizen. The disappearance of a firm, or a commercial bank, will become just a natural consequence of its lesser value to society. The central bank can then acquire full control over the contribution made by the financial system to encourage positive opportunistic behavior by economic agents.

But the success of the financial system depends a lot on the success of the investments made by entrepreneurs and, even though the investments may be a failure, society still needs to guarantee its own stability, as well as the persistence of entrepreneurs in their attempts at innovation.

#5 Creating an effective legal system

In chess, performing a double check happens when, with just one move, the player creates two threats against the opposing king, that is, two pieces give a check at the same time. Even if the threatened king's pieces can eliminate one of the attackers on the next move, there is still an opposing piece left that mates the king. As Anatoly Karpov points out, when faced with a double check, the king has only one recourse: to flee. In society, a judicial system is effective when people's negative opportunistic behavior is completely inhibited... And it can only run away!

There are many examples at our disposal to conclude about the ineffectiveness of the various legal systems existing in the world. As a result of the combination of our immense creativity and our bounded rationality, situations of abuse of power will be perpetrated whenever the established rules, and generally accepted by society, allow this to happen. Each person is able to identify a range of situations in which this occurs. However, much more often than it should happen, society allows people room to, rather than abuse a particular individual, abuse society in general. That is, in addition to situations of open conflict, in which one person seeks to achieve a position of dominance over another, there is, today, a space of indirect abuse to society in general, which is not intuitive.

This effort that human beings make, individually, to obtain a position of dominance over the rest of society, takes on the most diverse forms, legal and illegal. In legal forms, we can identify situations such as attempts to act in a cartel and the creation of barriers to the entry of other people in the same sector of economic activity, while venerating and stimulating competition in other sectors of activity. The world's economies are fertile in situations of this nature. In illegal forms, deliberate breaches of contract stand out. At this level, the examples also extend to society in general and often consist of attempts to reduce costs – on the part of producers, who provide worse customer service whenever they think that the consumer will not detect the situation – and in efforts of revenue increase. On the side of attempts to reduce costs, there are many examples such as the lack of hygiene in catering, the industrial use of raw materials of poorer quality than advertised, or the existence of monetary incentives for outsourcing service providers to adopt deceptive practices for the final consumer. On the side of efforts to increase revenues, we can identify the deliberate construction of products with reduced durability and, counter-intuitively, the postponement of payment terms to suppliers.

The last two practices, just mentioned in the previous paragraph, are highly harmful to the exercise of economic activity. In the first case, when producers intentionally manufacture products with reduced durability, they are contributing to a generalized increase in the consumption of natural resources without there being an effective need for this to happen. In the second case, when a company postpones payments for goods and services provided by its suppliers, it causes two negative consequences for society. On the one hand, it prevents these people from purchasing other goods and services from other members of the population. On the other hand, it uses this purchasing power to obtain business advantages. For example, let us imagine a construction company that hires a company of painters to paint a neighborhood of houses it has just built. Instead of paying for the painting firm in time, the construction firm managers use that money to buy new land where they plan to carry out another endeavor. In the acquisition of this new land, if the other construction companies fulfill their responsibilities, then the construction company that does not pay its suppliers on time will emerge, in this negotiation, with greater purchasing power than its competition. It is easy to see that the construction company of this example will acquire a dominant position in the construction market by virtue of an expedient that penalizes society as a whole and that has nothing to do with the quality of the service it provides. When these practices are generally adopted, society becomes unreliable.

The effectiveness of the legal system extends far beyond its ability to resolve conflicts between people, quickly and fairly. The effectiveness of the judicial system is defined, above all, by the way in which its operating rules induce positive opportunistic behavior in human beings.

When people mostly adopt negative opportunistic behaviors, the danger that this entails for the well-being of all of us is now very evident.

The notion of justice involves the concept of indemnity and the concept of compensation. Regardless of the technicality that the analysis of Law may confer on the two concepts, the truth is that we can define indemnity as the monetary value that the injured party in a given situation receives from the injuring party, and consider compensation as the way in which the injured party feels that he has recovered the same level of well-being he had before he was harmed. In the same way, justifying the concerns of the judicial system with the concept of equity, we can consider that compensation takes place when the wrongdoer feels an identical loss to the one he caused to the injured party.

Although it seems to be difficult to measure, the concept of compensation is assumed to be a determining bulwark of judicial equity. Indeed, by defining that the feeling of loss felt by the injured party must be identical to the feeling of loss caused to the injured party, the concept of compensation poses a difficulty for the legislator regarding the measurement of those feelings.

Within the scope of measuring the two feelings of compensation, Psychology has provided us with a decisive contribution to finding the right way for the judicial system to guarantee its effectiveness and provide a consistent stimulus to positive opportunistic behavior. Through the value function, Psychology demonstrates that the relationship between risk aversion, in the domain of gains, and preference for security, in the domain of losses, is, at least, two to one. In this context, if the breach of contract developed by the injured party is compensated by justice with the obligation to pay twice the loss it caused to the injured party, both will feel similarly at the end of the process. That is, the injured party will feel compensated for the loss that has been caused to him and the offender will feel that the attempt to obtain illegitimate gains is not justified. But Psychology, through the value function, also demonstrates that, faced with a rule of this kind, the human being starts to adopt a conscious and concerned posture of trying to avoid causing harm to third parties. This means that, if a breach of contract is dealt with in court with the obligation to indemnify the injured party for at least twice the quantifiable damage, justice takes a decisive step for society to achieve two desiderata: 1) every human being strive to avoid any breach of contract with third parties; and 2) in the event of litigation, as people do not know in advance how the judge will decide the dispute, people, in order to resolve the incident, will try to reach an understanding between themselves, for good, instead of hastily resorting to litigation, in bad faith.

The legal system is crucial to guarantee the predominance of positive opportunistic behaviors in human beings. When justice is limited to resorting to the concept of indemnity to repair emerging conflicts between people, we often find ourselves in situations where crime pays. People have room to act in bad faith. When society is capable of adequately compensating the injured parties, we reach a stage in which the effects of the negative situation inherent to the occurrence of a misfortune, which nobody wanted to happen, can be adequately minimized. People acquire a generalized certainty that everyone acts in good faith. Creating an effective legal system is crucial to making society more trustworthy.

#6 Striving for the "intelligent use of software"

Chess is an excellent demonstration platform that simply knowing the rules of a game is not enough for us to know how to play it well. Once we know the movement rules of each piece well, it is the use we give to the pieces that allow us to increase or reduce the potential that each one has to be decisive for the final outcome of the game. One of the exercises of this nature, which the chess beginner learns from an early age, consists in understanding the power of the combined use of the two rooks. The chess game can be won when the two rooks harmoniously combine in successive moves on the seventh rank.

The five rules for moving society identified above – enact full employment; prevent the use of real guarantees in granting credit; prevent the creation of money to grant consumer credit; guarantee that the creation of money is destined to investment credit; and create an effective legal system - they all need to resort to the intelligent use of software to be effective. We realize that global society is in competition with itself, in a permanent effort to consolidate positive opportunistic behaviors and inhibit negative opportunistic behaviors. However, once again, the intensification of the use of technology stirs up, in many people, the fear of loss. Concretely, given the experience felt in the past, the fear that human beings have regarding the possibility of losing their job to a robot will be a social foundation of resistance to its implementation. This fear of fostering the "intelligent use of software" is an adversary that must be faced.

Our current society provides many examples of attempts to win the game without the rational analysis process having been well established. Two of these examples are given by the effort to protect intellectual property and the attempt to avoid fraud in the insurance business.

In 1421, in Florence, Italy, an individual invented a device to transport marble and realized that he could only guarantee a high profit from the exploitation of that idea if the rest of society was prevented from building similar devices. So, he convinced the local government to recognize his copyright and ensure the exploitation of his invention on an exclusive basis, during a given period of time. Later, in 1474, in Venice, Italy, the first exploration license appeared. But it was only in 1790, in the United

States, that a country passed a patent law that guaranteed its inventor the right to exploit his invention under a monopoly regime.

This was the first move on the part of the inventor – getting society to protect him in order to provide him with an incentive to continue to innovate. Cumulatively, society realized that, by doing so, the patent falls into public knowledge. This situation allows for its improvement and awakens the rest of society to other related inventive possibilities. Despite being aware that the inventor is provided the possibility of exploiting the rest of society with his invention, the rule of exclusivity is created in order to reap benefits that may exceed this cost.

But, this was just the first move. And positive opportunistic behavior is followed by negative opportunistic behavior.

Let us first analyze the effects on society arising from the current patent registration rules. Specifically, an individual who conceives an unprecedented product, which is not a mere combination of existing techniques, and whose invention has recognized practical applicability, can register his patent to ensure that the disclosure, manufacture, and exploitation of the invention will be controlled by themselves, during a perfectly defined period of time.

Basically, we have two types of patents. The invention patent, which fully fits the above definition and usually has a duration of twenty years, and the utility model, which reflects the creation of improvements applied to existing products and has a usual duration of ten years. In essence, the registration of patents aims to create an incentive for people to get involved in research and development activities of new technologies, and be duly rewarded for this effort. It is intended to ensure that society will enjoy a greater number of inventions available than those that would supposedly happen in the absence of this mechanism. It is intended to encourage positive opportunistic behavior.

However, in practice, and given that an opportunity is simply a favorable circumstance that is taken advantage of by those with executive power to act immediately in the face of perceived conditions, the effects of the use of patents under the economy's current rules of operation can have negative harmful effects.

It is perfectly clear that the inventor can only benefit from the invention if one of two circumstances occurs:

either the individual has the financial power to properly exploit his invention or the person is forced to sell his invention to the highest bidder he can get within a certain period of time. In the first case, the existence of the patent registration mechanism, as it currently operates, becomes redundant. Society will always benefit from the invention regardless of the existence of a patent protection record. In the second case, in which the inventor is unable to place his creation on the market and has to sell it to those who can, this invention is acquired by those who are already active in that market niche with other products. In this situation, the new invention is often put on hold and, instead of being acquired to be commercialized, it is acquired to prevent its commercialization. The purchaser only intends to prevent other people from competing with the obsolete and lower-quality products that he is already selling in the market. The acquirer adopts negative opportunistic behavior, which harms society, and which harms him the greater the number of these actions that are replicated by other people in society.

A patent registration mechanism is a tool through which society tries to encourage the individual who "can" be creative, to actually be so. However, as always happens when we are faced with institutional processes that seek to condition citizens' choices, opportunities open up, in the positive and negative sense, and their final effects are only fully understood when society engages in attitudes of cooperation.

There are now numerous useful inventions put on hold. Cumulatively, there are companies that identify useful inventions and wait for them to expire in order to use them. The registration of a patent, or utility model, requires the payment of an annual fee to maintain the protection of the intellectual property of its inventor, and this protection expires in the absence of payment or at the end of the protection periods of twenty, or ten years, respectively. In addition to gross violations of the intellectual property protection mechanism, which can only be resolved in court, this form of action by society also does not have the desired positive opportunistic behavior that was intended to be achieved when the idea of protecting intellectual property arose. Negative opportunistic behavior has also played its part.

The technological evolution of society allows us to find increasingly rational ways of controlling society's emotional reactions. The creation of legislation on the use of patents and utility models raised the need to adapt control and penalization mechanisms, to avoid conceding them immediate ineffectiveness. A first need arose to demand obedience. Later, even scrupulously obeying what the law advocates, some companies acquire an invention to prevent it from being placed on the market to compete with their current products. Society founds perverse ways of using the law. And it is this fantastic ability of human beings to take advantage of opportunities, in the positive and negative senses, which leads us to progress when we have the humility to realize that there is a continuous need for attention and adaptation. Today, the intelligent use of software makes it possible for global society to take another step toward progress.

The aim is the continuous use of human genius. Thus, to duly reward the inventive effort, while encouraging the putting into practice of each new invention, in the shortest possible time, we can resort to the "intelligent use of software," and make a new move, in a positive mode.

Today, it is possible to create a central register of patents and utility models, assigning each new invention a unique registration, with its dissemination shared on a global scale. Cumulatively, given the advanced state of technology, it is also possible to guarantee that each unit's use of the invention provides its creator with an income. For example, for each unit sold of a good using this invention, the inventor will receive one cent, or one euro, or ten, or whatever the inventor determines. Now, instead of guaranteeing the inventor temporary exploitation under a monopoly regime, which only works well when the inventor has the financial capacity to exploit his invention, we can guarantee that all people who want to do so can also exploit the invention. And do it right away. On the one hand, the inventor, who does not have the financial capacity to exploit his invention, no longer needs to sell it to be rewarded for his effort. On the other hand, the investor, with the financial capacity to exploit an invention, does not have to pay in advance for his exploitation right. Neither the inventor runs the risk of selling his patent at a price too low, nor the investor is forced to take a risk too high in buying an invention that he does not know yet if it will be successful on the market. The development of technology allows humanity to go much further than what we have done so far.

A second example, clarifying the importance of the "intelligent use of software" for the progress of humanity, comes from the insurance activity.

The insurance contract is based on society's consistent observation that negative and unpleasant situations can happen to anyone. It is said that the first insurance contract emerged during the time of the Phoenicians, between 1500 BC. and 300 BC.. The Phoenicians were merchant people, very connected to the sea. As a result of their maritime commercial culture, these people loaded galleys, propelled by sail and oars, with goods produced in a given location and carried out commercial exchanges with people from other regions. The galleys returned home loaded with other supplies necessary for the survival of the local people. However, from time to time, one or another galley would be caught in a storm and sunk. When that happened, the survival of the families of the owners of those goods was difficult. As these accidents could happen to any galley, it is said that the local people created a mechanism to protect society. It consisted of building a warehouse where each ship placed a small percentage of its cargo before departure. If any ship went to the bottom, the existing cargo in that warehouse was destined for the families of unfortunate sailors who did not return. Allegedly, this is how the first insurance "contract" emerged.

More or less jokingly, more or less seriously, it is also said that with him came the fraud. And once or twice, an empty galley left the starting point...

On the positive side, and more seriously, the insurance contract consists of society's effort to set aside a little of its income to face the misfortune of whoever it may be, ours or that of others. Insurers, aware that fraud is a possible human behavior in taking advantage of detected opportunities, seek to create defensive processes. The most common is the increase in the price of insurance contracts when the customer reports a claim. The insurer uses its software to make sure that the customer, who has presented a claim under an insurance contract, will now have to pay more in future periods. In extreme cases, insurers even denounce insurance contracts and refuse to accept those people as their clients. In these situations, insurers act negatively, based on their fear of being the target of fraud.

The use of the software by the insurance industry is to create a database that allows identifying customers who report claims and ensuring that the insurance industry is able to do one of two things: 1) or force these people to pay more for insurance; and 2) or prevent them from having access to this protection. For some people, it makes sense that fraud should be punished. For other people, it makes sense that those who gave "loss" to the insurer have to pay more than the others. However, this boundedly rational way of acting does not benefit any member of society.

Society always suffers a loss, whether when the price of insurance is increased in the event of a claim, or when the insurer refuses to take out an insurance contract for someone who registers an "exaggerated" loss ratio. As the Phoenicians did, insurance was created so that everyone can contribute a little to ensure everyone's protection, especially when misfortune strikes. The greater the number of paying people, the lower the price to pay to guarantee this protection. The price of insurance is given by the average number of claims verified in a given period of time, multiplied by the average cost of each claim, and added by a profit margin to pay the insurer's work. The more people with a current contract, the lower the price the insurer can charge. Therefore, whenever the insurer increases the price of insurance for a customer who has an accident, it is just making him go looking for another insurer, no longer being protected, or having less financial availability to take out other insurance contracts. In any of these three situations, because the cost of the insurer's work does not change, the price of the insurance portfolio must rise. Members of society are left to pay more for each insurance contract. Society is less protected if no other insurer accepts the insurance contract at a lower price. And the insurer that engages in this practice becomes less competitive in the market. Everyone loses.

The use of software can be much smarter if it is used positively. The insurance contract exists so that we are all protected if misfortune befalls any of us. But, we know that fraud exists. We know that irresponsibility also exists. Thus, we intend to inhibit negative opportunistic behaviors through which one or another member of society seeks to take advantage of the rest, even though he is aware that he himself lives worse if everyone else does the same. However, we also realize that we will have to get insurance contracts as cheaply as possible and spread across as many people in society as possible. Once again, we move away from intuitive thoughts triggered by emotion and are forced to deepen our reasoning in the sequential evolution of future plays.

In the insurance business, fraud usually arises when

damage occurs and the person has not yet been protected against this possibility by means of an insurance contract. Continuing this line of reasoning, the lower the price of insurance, the greater the number of situations in which the amount of damage is greater than the price to be paid for the protection; that is, the lower the insurance price, the greater the possibility of profitable fraud for the perpetrator. But this is reasoning based on fear. And, the higher the price of insurance, the smaller the number of people in society who can enjoy this protection. Negative opportunistic behavior wins the game when fear prevails.

At first glance, distributing as many insurance contracts as we can at the lowest possible price is a measure that might even seem like an invitation to fraud. However, on the positive side, we are creating a rule that defines the insurance contract and we try to ensure that it is as widely disseminated throughout society as possible because protection is a win-win situation for everyone. Attentive to negative opportunistic behavior, we realize that this process can be explored individually because, as human beings, boundedly rational but immensely creative, we recognize that we all have these capabilities. Thus, as a society, we cannot do without the benefits that the positive side of the insurance contract brings us and we have to inhibit negative opportunistic behavior. It is therefore necessary to reduce the reward for negative opportunistic behavior.

In this sense, instead of seeking to charge more for contracts that show claims, insurers should adopt a rule in which the indemnity to be received by the insured will be successively lower, the greater the number of claims that the individual presents. For example, a more effective rule than increasing the price of insurance in the event of a claim consists of reducing a percentage of the indemnity for each claim submitted previously by the customer, in the last three years. For example, we can define that the indemnity to be received by the customer will be deducted from 10% of the losses calculated for each claim that has been made to the insurers before that occurrence. In this way, the first claim will be fully compensated. The second claim will be compensated at 90%, the third at 80%, and so on... Because people do not know when misfortune happens, nor how big it is, the prospect of being able to be left unprotected in about 10% of the indemnifiable losses, of a misfortune that cannot be quantified in advance, will make the person only report a first claim when in fact needs the protection. And the idea of being reduced to 20% after the first claim constitutes a very strong additional stimulus for the insurer's customer to avoid the first claim right away. In addition, the cheaper the insurance, the greater the number of people who take out the insurance to ensure protection. The need for oversight is greatly reduced because fraud is reduced by customer initiative. The customer's responsibility for preventing claims also increases significantly. The insurer can trust because the rule makes the customer more reliable. This second regulatory mechanism, instead of being based on penalty and fear, obtains its effectiveness by outstanding the reward.

Worldwide, insurers have created computer software to record car accidents verified by license plate and the policyholder. Notably, and regrettably, insurers have made a concerted effort to manage to charge a higher price to all citizens who have previously registered claims throughout the territory. However, the reality is that the risk of a car accident is exactly the same for an experienced driver who had an accident yesterday and for the same experienced driver a few months ago. Effectively, the occurrence of an accident can even confer a future risk reduction because the human being learns from making mistakes. But, due to a lack of focus and hardships in the deepening of reasoning, the insurance industry resorts to using software to penalize this same customer after the accident. The intelligent use of software will always be a challenge for humanity.

The development of technology allows an ever greater use of human creativity. If this capacity is used with a focus on the advantages that it can bring to society, we will be in a position to create a prosperous and reliable institutional environment, where every human being sees positive opportunistic behavior stimulated and negative opportunistic behavior inhibited.

Today we live in a reality in which technology helps us to overcome many fears. In a very specific way, the "blockchain" technology – a chain of blocks – allows the sharing of data through an information network interconnected in the chain. The way this data string is linked is what makes it reliable. The technology ensures that the data is chronologically consistent because it is not possible to delete or modify the data without the network's consent. Thus, any attempt to modify the data requires joint authorization from the network elements. The technology is therefore based on decentralizing the validation of operations. There is no presence of a supervisory entity, which would mean creating a point of vulnerability. By making each operation validated simultaneously by the entire network, or by a large and random number of participants in the network, "blockchain" technology constitutes a tamper-proof mechanism. Given that the data has multiple storage and verification spaces, whenever someone, outside the network, tries to introduce a change in the data recorded in a given location, this tampering attempt will be detected because the data will be inconsistent with other locations and will not be consensually validated by other network participants. Blockchain technology does not inhibit negative opportunistic behavior but allows its immediate detection, prevents its negative effects, and prevents its proliferation.

The "blockchain" technology is at the basis of the creation and development of digital currencies precisely because it has these characteristics that give it great security in the execution of financial operations. This security allows the financial sector to eliminate the need to undertake financial reconciliation operations to ensure the correctness of data on file. But other sectors of economic activity have also embraced technology. In retail and large-scale distribution, companies use "blockchain" technology to monitor the movement of goods between sellers and buyers and ensure the integrity of contracts. In the management of intellectual property rights, companies linked to the media and entertainment use "blockchain" technology to ensure correct contractual compliance with the amounts agreed upon for sales of content developed by artists – musicians, writers, etc. In health, the electronic medical record was developed and the Telemedicine sector is developing at full speed. Blockchain is a technology that helps humans overcome their limitations in detecting negative opportunistic behavior and leverages our creativity to spur positive opportunistic behavior.

Society's insecurity increases when people depend on centralized processes. These situations reduce our possibility of success. A simple example comes from the recent pandemic crisis caused by Covid-19. Specifically, the World Health Organization, based in the United Nations, took the lead in the process on a global scale. There was a clear situation in which an individual, an organization, or a group, framed in a well-defined hierarchical structure, exercised its power in an arbitrary way, and imposed conditions on the entire world population. Consequently, the awareness of this reality, combined with our limitations in accessing and understanding the little information that was coming to us, made it make sense to think that this was a situation in which some human beings abused the rights, freedoms, and guarantees of everyone else. In other words, the conspiracy theory will always make sense when there is a centralized control that imposes its will. And this situation does not contribute to society winning the game.

The "software" has been used by humanity to supply the most diverse limitations that the human being has in the execution of the tasks that he proposes to do. Among these, we can identify the need to stimulate positive opportunistic behaviors and inhibit negative opportunistic behaviors. Using technology to increase our capabilities in this domain will be like getting both rooks into action on the seventh row. Consequently, the "intelligent use of software" is a fundamental step towards consolidating a virtuous society, in which behaviors of respect, tolerance, and understanding will prevail.

#7 Abolishing borders and granting the free

movement of people, goods, and capital

The good chess player protects all his pieces and is willing to sacrifice his Queen to win the game. Cumulatively, as the game unfolds and the balance between the position of each player is dominant, a player can decide the dispute in his favor if he manages to promote a Pawn to Queen, that is, if the player manages to get a Pawn to reach the other end of the board. For a chess player, all pieces are important in order to win the game.

Despite the many examples that history has already provided, and which are headed by Pisistratus, the importance of each human being for the well-being of the remaining ones is something that humanity has not yet learned to properly value. But the economic and social development of Athens constitutes empirical data on how the well-being of a society depends on the joint action of many individuals who specialize in the activities that each one does best. Indeed, even if some people are not capable of doing anything better than others, the well-being of society depends on the joint action of all individuals. And there we are before a concept that is not intuitive.

In the mid-nineteenth century, the economist David Ricardo explained to the world that a country has an advantage in developing trade with another country, even when that other country is not capable of producing anything as well as ours. The economist explained that, for there to be advantages in the trade of goods between the two countries, it is enough that there is a situation of comparative advantage in the production of a certain good. Quantifying the idea with a numerical example helps a lot to clarify the pertinence, and importance, of the author's conclusion.

As a hypothesis, let us consider two countries, "A" and "B", and two products, "P1" and "P2", both equally valuable to the populations of countries "A" and "B". Let us assume that country "A" manages to produce two units of "P1" for each hour of work, and the same happens in relation to the production of "P2". Let us assume that the productivity of country "B" is lower than country "A" both in the production of "P1" and in the production of "P2". Concretely, for each hour of work, country "B" manages to produce one unit of "P1" and only half a unit of "P2".

In this context, we can draw up a table with the total daily production of the two countries assuming that both share eight hours of work per day for the production of "P1" and "P2" and that, in both countries, people value the benefit of diversity – that is, people prefer to have "rice" and "pasta" rather than having to go through the feeling "rice again!…". Thus, in country "A", at the end of a working day, eight units of "P1" and eight units of "P2" were produced, corresponding to four hours of work dedicated to each product multiplied by the productivity of two units per hour. In turn, in country "B", analogously, and at the end of a working day, four units of "P1" and two units of "P2" were obtained. The joint production of the two countries reaches 22 units of the two equally valuable products for their populations (from "A" = 8+8 and from "B" = 4+2).

Although country "B" is worse than country "A" in the production of both products, both have the opportunity to obtain productivity gains if each one specializes in the production of the good that it produces comparatively better. In this example, with regard to product "P1", country "A" produces two units per hour while country "B" is capable of producing only one. Therefore, country "A" is twice as good as country "B" in producing "P1". As for product "P2", country "A" produces two units per hour while country "B" is capable of producing only half a unit. So, in the production of "P2", country "A" is four times better than country "B". Therefore, country "A" has a comparative advantage in the production of "P2". If country "A" specializes in the production of "P2" and country "B" specializes in the production of "P1", each country specializes in the production of the product it does comparatively better, and then, together, the two countries reach a total production of 24 units.

This productivity gain, which is obtained as a result of comparative specialization, is not intuitive, but it is extremely important that its awareness is acquired. As Marilyn vos Savant demonstrated in the "Monty Hall" problem, human beings have bounded rationality, but they learn to think. If global society understands that it is possible to produce more, work less, and live in peace to enjoy prosperity, what reason could there be for it not to do so?

David Ricardo disclosed this precious information approximately one hundred and fifty years ago. It unequivocally demonstrates that the opening of borders to the free movement of people and goods constitutes, in itself, a factor of prosperity and well-being. However, over time, economics has developed numerous studies on the subject. Until today, these studies have not been able to gather unanimity as to the contribution that the opening of the economies of each country provides for an effective improvement in the living conditions of the populations.

In 2011, professor and Italian economist, Pierluigi Montalbano, dealing with the issue of opening up the economies of different countries, pointed out that external shocks caused by the hand of governments, through the adoption of certain legal frameworks, often leave the poorer members of society unprotected against the adverse effects that may result from this and, also, less prepared to take advantage of opportunities, compared to what happens to the richest people in those same countries. Consequently, in the economy, in addition to the emergence of behaviors aimed at obtaining productivity gains that come from the opening of borders, other types of behavior are developed with the aim of taking immediate advantage of the situation. And the final result for the population is the sum of the consequences of these actions. This fact explains the lack of unanimity in the conclusions of the numerous studies carried out regarding the pertinence of opening an economy to the outside world. Although humanity is aware of the prosperity that can come from eliminating impediments to the free movement of people, goods, and capital, the power of our many fears, in conjunction with our bounded rationality, has prevented us from definitively embracing positive opportunistic behaviors and adequately deal with negative opportunistic behaviors.

<u>Specialization gains in the production of equally valued goods</u>

1- Units produced / Hour of work

Country / Product	P1	P2
A	2.00	2.00
B	1.00	0.50

2- Allocation of working time by product, WITHOUT specialization (in hours)

Country / Product	P1	P2
A	4.00	4.00
B	4.00	4.00

3- Production/day (8 hours of work), WITHOUT specialization (=1x2)

Country / Product	P1	P2
A	8.00	8.00
B	4.00	2.00

Result	A+B	22.00

4- Allocation of working time by product, WITH specialization (in hours)

Country / Product	P1	P2
A	0.00	8.00
B	8.00	0.00

5- Production/day (8 hours of work), WITH specialization (=1x4)

Country / Product	P1	P2
A	0.00	16.00
B	8.00	0.00

Result	A+B	24.00

Note: Based on Sousa, A. (1988) "Análise económica"

The effects of opening borders are positive, both for

rich countries and for poor countries. Angola is a country rich in natural resources. But, this ability does not adequately translate into prosperity for its people. Especially, the country has diamonds, petroleum, iron, copper, manganese, mica, phosphate, lead, tin, gold, silver, and platinum. In addition to minerals, it also has coffee, cattle, arable land, and important fishing resources. Angola is a country with 1,247,000 square kilometers. It's a territory bigger than Portugal, Spain, and France all put together. The population of Angola has approximately 35 million inhabitants and is less than a third of the population of Portugal, Spain, and France, which together exceed 125 million people. The Gross Domestic Product (GDP) of Angola, in 2021, was 1,652 euros per inhabitant. Also in 2021, for Portugal, Spain, and France, the respective GDP per capita was 20,772 euros for Portugal, 25,453 euros for Spain, and 36,915 euros for France. In material terms, the population of Portugal, Spain, and France lives many times better than the population of Angola. If the free movement of people, goods, and capital is implemented between a country like Angola and other countries like Portugal, Spain, and France, then the know-how of each individual will be directed toward taking advantage of every identified opportunity. And all people are important in the process: Angolans, Portuguese, Spanish, and French.

The chess player cannot do without a pawn. Ultimately, to win the game, the individual can only enter into a process of exchanges whose sequence will lead to an advantageous final result for the player with greater depth of reasoning. For our global society to be successful, it also needs to adopt positive opportunistic behaviors. And a fundamental step is to leave no one behind.

Checkmate

One of the hardest lessons to learn in chess is that achieving checkmate usually requires great care and preparation. Even when a player has a clear advantage on the board, the opponent can still tie the game if he manages to reach the situation of "perpetual check" or "draw due to drowning". The situation of "perpetual check" happens when the player at a disadvantage manages to find a way to threaten the opponent's king with a check, leaving only one escape square to the king in advantage. When the king in advantage flees to the only available square, the player in disadvantage again checks this position, forcing the king in advantage to flee again to the initial square. Since this situation has no end, the game is considered a tie. The situation of "draw for drowned" happens when, cumulatively, three things happen: 1) the king of the player in disadvantage is not in check; 2) any move the king of the player in disadvantage can make would put it in check; and 3) it is not possible for the disadvantaged player to move any piece other than the king. The search for the "draw for drowning" situation leads to the game being prolonged even when the material disadvantage of a player is enormous. For him, the hope persists of still being able to avoid defeat by taking advantage of an eventual slip by the opponent. Therefore, whatever advantage a player has in the game, failure can knock at the door, at any time, through a small distraction.

So that human society can overcome the challenge it has with itself, it is necessary to be aware of our rational limitations, our fears, and how high the possibility of failure is if we do not prepare properly to prevent it from happening. The creation of a reliable society, in which each human being naturally adopts positive opportunistic behaviors and inhibits himself from practicing negative opportunistic behaviors, is something that is not intuitive, it is not immediate to be achieved, and it is also not easy to reach. But it is possible.

The first step is to implement a full-employment society. It is the first step towards leaving no one behind. It is the first step for society to assume itself as one and healthy, instead of divided and sick.

The advantages of a full-employment society are many, but there are some positive consequences for all, which are not intuitive and deserve to be highlighted.

One of the most salient advantages of the full-employment society is its power to solve the problem of pollution. Today, we live in a reality in which society does not guarantee employment for the entire active population, and, in order to survive, people need to sell the goods and services they produce. Given that companies compete with each other for consumer preference, and consumers prefer to pay as little as possible for the products they consume, then no company can, lightly, stop trying to produce at the lowest possible cost. If the production costs have to involve carrying out large investments, destined to eliminate the pollution that the company's economic activity causes, these investments will represent a threatening increase in costs and one of two things will happen: 1) either the profit decreases if the company maintains its selling price; 2) or the selling price has to increase and the company will lose competitiveness in the market. Consequently, in today's society, where profit is the entrepreneur's dominant concern because their survival depends on it, companies are not inclined to willingly embrace non-polluting practices whenever this represents an increase in their production costs.

However, given the implementation of the full-employment society, profit tends to be zero, and for each entrepreneur, and each worker, everyone will only care about the size of their salary. The survival of each human being no longer depends on having to make a profit with what is produced, but rather on having to produce well. An entrepreneur will have the option of closing his small, unproductive, and polluting company and going to work for a larger company where he can earn a salary at least equal to the remuneration he derives from operating his business. The full-employment society gives people the option of being employees or employers, according to the function in which they feel they can be most useful. The full-employment society is a wage-maximizing society, and this factor alone provides society with the certainty that its members can commit themselves to eliminating pollution.

In 2010, professor and economist Antoinette Schoar highlighted the differences between subsistence entrepreneurship, which occurs in most developing economies, and transformational entrepreneurship, which allows society to reach truly high levels of productivity. By making it possible for people to choose to be employers or employees, the full-employment society will make companies tend to be larger, take advantage of economies of scale, and be increasingly efficient in their production processes. Today, transformational entrepreneurship lacks an institutional foundation that allows people to be naturally driven to adopt positive opportunistic behaviors.

There are more advantages to consider that are somewhat not intuitive. One of them lies in the freedom that firms now have to set the sale price they see fit. With the rules for implementing full employment, society is able to shelter monopoly firms, in the sense of being the only operators in the market, without this representing any kind of loss for the remaining citizens. Today, the monopoly firm takes advantage of society by setting a sale price far above its production cost, providing the remaining members of society with a small quantity of product, compared to the total quantities it manages to produce. But, with the rules for implementing full employment, the most profitable firms will be the first to receive unemployed people. Soon, entrepreneurs will be aware that profits will be momentary if they maintain the commercial policy of "high price-low production" for too long. In 1977, professors and economists, Avinash K. Dixit and Joseph E. Stiglitz – the latter was awarded the Nobel Prize in Economics in 2001 – stressed that society benefits from a greater diversity of products available when firms adopt practices of monopolistic competition. That is, when, in the market, firms seek to be monopolists in a certain niche, society will have at its disposal a greater number of goods. Some firms are dedicated to the manufacture of chocolate, others to the manufacture of candies, others to the manufacture of biscuits, and so on, and the community benefits from a greater diversity of sweets to consume. At full employment, monopoly firms that adopt this type of practice, regardless of charging prices as high as the demand for them allows, induce an ever greater business specialization in specific market niches. Cumulatively, firms will maximize their workers' wages. Naturally, the income of firms is distributed among the active population as a result of the effort put into practices of monopolistic competition. The selling price of products decreases as society's overall income is distributed over an ever-increasing number of products, which are often substitutes for one another. Society can thus trust that the selling price of goods available to the community is as low as possible, without needing to depend on the quality, and capacity for action, of the authorities created in each country to guarantee competition between firms.

These rules are in line with the explanation given in 1776 by Adam Smith regarding society's interest in allowing the producer to freely set his price. The author explained that the functioning of the free market, allowing producers to arbitrarily decide the selling price of their products, is crucial for the well-being of populations because it naturally adjusts the quantities consumed and produced. The author mentions, with simplicity and mastery, the example of the price of corn. In a year of good harvest, in which many tons of corn can be distributed among the population, the unit price of corn can be lower, keeping the producer his income. In a year of bad harvest, in which the tons of corn to be distributed by the population are now much smaller, the price of corn has to be much higher. In this way, society guarantees that corn consumption, over time, will be done gradually and appropriately for its availability. This avoids the extreme hunger that could arise if the rate of consumption of unit amounts of corn were to remain the same in a year of bad harvest as if it were a year of good harvest. Additionally, by guaranteeing the farmer's income in the year of bad harvest, society also guarantees that the producer remains active for the following year. In our case, implementing full employment with the rules defined in the first move, we guarantee that even the price practiced by a monopoly firm is the one that best serves the interests of the community.

Another advantage of implementing a full-employment society is the possibility of completely eradicating the negative effect of taxes on society. This does not mean that there is no need to exchange some of our work for the work of those who build and maintain roads, clean our streets, or who safeguard water, electricity, communications, security, and education supplies. But these companies, whether publicly or privately owned, only have to exist as long as they are useful and can be closed whenever they are no longer necessary, without resulting in the possibility of compromising anyone's survival. And, also, without this representing a decrease in aggregate demand for the goods and services produced in the economy.

With the implementation of the full-employment society, people acquire the ability to refuse to harm others, even if they receive an express order to do so. The fact that there is no longer any fear of saying goodbye, or being fired, gives employees the ability to do what their conscience dictates. With the survival and quality of life of the entire population completely assured, society can now say "NO" to negative opportunistic behavior. And to do it voluntarily. Pharmaceuticals are now able to stop producing medicines that only suppress the unpleasant effects of symptoms instead of providing a definitive cure for the patient; car manufacturers are now able to build reliable, long-lasting vehicles, instead of weakening the durability of components to force customers to make frequent purchases in the future; mechanic workshops can now be honest about the work they do on their customers' cars; bakers can now avoid labeling a cake made yesterday as having been made today; teachers are no longer afraid that students will film their classes; strikes cease to exist because they are now completely useless; politicians can stop lying; etc; etc; etc. Society becomes more reliable, not because the rules say so, but because each customer knows that the people who are selling a good or providing a service do not depend on deceptive actions to survive.

The implementation of a full-employment society is the only process through which the problems of scarcity, poverty, and inequality can be dealt with efficiently. Despite the fact that they are three different situations, the common citizen tends to consider that they are the same thing. On the one hand, society's productivity is only at its maximum when it operates at full employment. Therefore, society acquires a greater capacity to avoid the situation of scarcity. Secondly, the existence of situations of extreme poverty only persists because society exhibits problems in the distribution of available resources among the members of its population. At full employment, the distribution of products across the entire active population is automatically ensured. Lastly, social inequality is the simple manifestation of the dominance of negative opportunistic behaviors by some members of society over others. Our bounded rationality prevents us from being deeply aware of our difficulties. But the implementation of a full-employment society gives a decisive help for us to be successful.

Despite the importance of all the above, the most salient advantage of the full-employment society is its ability to eradicate the occurrence of economic crises. As pointed out by Milton Friedman, Nobel Prize in Economics in 1976, an economic crisis is always a period of scarcity in the midst of abundance. It is a period when people are starving and there are human and material resources to be used. It is also a period of social crisis that underlines our bounded rationality and highlights our difficulties in organizing ourselves properly as a global community.

Economic crises can arise for only three reasons: 1) the withdrawal of money from the economy; 2) the decrease in consumption on the part of aggregate demand; and 3) the reduction of production by aggregate supply. Society controls all these possibilities if it implements the seven moves that allow it to control the negative opportunistic behavior of its members. However, the eradication of any economic crisis from society needs further clarification.

First, in the current institutional environment, whenever the financial system withdraws money from the economy, people have less purchasing power to purchase the goods produced by companies at market prices. Consequently, companies stop selling all their production. In this reality, in order to survive, entrepreneurs feel that they have to produce less, reduce wages, fire people, or implement a combination of these three management measures. Any of these measures will imply an additional reduction in the aggregate demand that is directed to the goods produced by companies. And the economic crisis is consolidated. In a society of full employment, this negative vicious cycle is stopped, right from the start, by the fact that we build a society where full employment is always guaranteed. The fact that people continue to work, that entrepreneurs can adjust wages whenever they see fit, and that companies do not have incentives to reduce production with the sole purpose of ensuring profit levels, makes society permanently ensure the highest levels of aggregate demand it manages to maintain. Therefore, companies can also maintain production levels at maximum capacity. And that prevents the negative economic cycle from having any possibility of occurring.

Secondly, and in the same way, if society is satisfied with the consumption of a certain good, or set of goods, it can dispense with the forced, and useless, production of additional quantities. People who are employed in that economic activity move on to another, and their knowledge and skills continue to be useful to society without a general decrease in the purchasing power of aggregate demand. The economy adjusts its quantities and prices, within normal limits, without stress, without setbacks, and without provoking any additional stimulus to consolidate a negative economic cycle.

Finally, whenever companies reduce production and charge higher prices, they will immediately create opportunities for other people to dedicate themselves to these economic activities, employ the people who have just been laid off and cancel out that negative economic impulse. If the action is intentional, these monopoly behaviors can no longer trigger future additional negative consequences for society. If the action is not deliberate, as, for example, if the reduction in production is caused by a phenomenon of nature, then society naturally embarks on the necessary and adequate adjustments to restore the living conditions of all people, without leaving no one outside.

The full-employment society, based on the seven moves identified above, makes it possible to protect society against the possibility of any economic crisis. We will build a society that laughs. We will build a society that supports each other whenever a misfortune arises.

The full-employment society is a decisive step towards making positive opportunistic behaviors dominant – those that make us all live better the more times they are replicated by other people.

We saw that the positioning of our pieces needs careful preparation if we intend to conclude the game with a successful final checkmate. The implementation of the full-employment society requires adjustments to the various institutional processes on which our daily behavior is based. It is these adjustments that consolidate a set of advantages that are often not intuitive for us.

The abolition of the use of collateral in credit operations is one of the fundamental adjustments. First, access to credit operations is generalized to all people in general, regardless of their prior wealth. Second, banks are starting to focus their decision-making process on their perception of the quality of the business plan under analysis and are not distracted by real estate interests, or of any other nature, divergent from the economic activity carried out by the customer. Third, in case of temporary difficulties for the firms, instead of the banks being inflexible and forcing the collection of the real guarantees, leaving the entrepreneur without solutions, the banks start to have an effective motivation to review the negotiation conditions of their credits whenever the business of the client presents future viability. Fourth, the very cost of producing a bank credit operation decreases. There are fewer records, less bureaucracy, less difficulty in negotiations, and faster response to customer requests. Society, as a whole, stands to gain from the abolition of collateral in credit operations.

The third move, to position society to consistently stimulate positive opportunistic behavior, is to prevent the creation of money for granting consumer credit. This measure entails two major advantages for society. One, it contributes decisively to preventing the worsening of pay inequalities between employers and employees. Another, it ensures that people's savings are duly remunerated by the financial system. It should be noted that, if any of these moves do not materialize, because we leave an open space for negative opportunistic behaviors to happen, we run a serious risk of not winning the game.

The fourth move is to ensure that new money creation is exclusively devoted to investment credit. By creating new money, the financial system is raising its own purchasing power in the future and immediately increasing the purchasing power of entrepreneurs who may sell their already-made products at a higher price. But, by certifying that this additional purchasing power is intended only for entrepreneurs, society guarantees that this privilege, which some happy entrepreneurs will now receive, is intended to increase the number of products and services available to everyone, at lower prices. Banks are, once again, encouraged to prioritize good business ideas regardless of the prior material wealth that proponents of credit operations already have. With this move, we guarantee that the positive dynamics of entrepreneurship will be within everyone's reach. Simultaneously, the continuous application of the use of immense human creativity will also always be present in our societies. Finally, we managed to make negative opportunistic behaviors no longer make sense. The use of acts of bribery, influence peddling, or other practices aimed at an individual, organization, or group to take an illegitimate advantage in society ceases because the bank will only be focused on the success and analysis of each business idea. And nothing else. Society becomes reliable, not because there is a tight inspection that allows it to conclude, not because there is a certifying entity that says so, not because there is a friend who affirms it, but because we know, without a doubt, that people's motivation is solely directed towards adopting positive opportunistic behaviors because negative opportunistic behaviors have become absurd.

Our fifth move aims to further elevate the absurdity of adopting negative opportunistic behaviors. A legal system is effective when all members of society at large realize that crime does not pay. For a crime to be rewarding, we have to raise some considerations: 1) is the person who commits a crime above the law?; 2) is the law providing for a penalty of lesser value than the reward that the crime provides?; and 3) is justice slow, inattentive, or ineffective, which allows the practitioner of a crime to get away unharmed? Some of these issues begin to be resolved with the full-employment situation.

With the implementation of the full-employment society, according to the rules identified above, the companies or activities with the highest profit will be the first to be pressured to share these profits with their employees. Therefore, a crime of an economic nature automatically becomes less rewarding because society has a natural corrective mechanism if the information relating to the profits of operations is duly registered. Likewise, it will make less and less sense that there is someone above the law because people become more and more equal in accessing the opportunities that social life affords them. Finally, the incentive for society to reject the existence of criminals, who harm others, increases, because everyone becomes aware that no one has the need to act in a way that harms other people for their own benefit. However, an effective legal system has to be fast, and active, to be of recognized utility to society.

The consolidation of this certainty is only acquired when the breach of contract is deliberately avoided by the parties involved in a process. Today, conflicts proliferate in society because crime pays off. A client told me one day that "papers were made to safeguard good intentions." And he was right. It is with the care of translating into writing what people think that it is possible to avoid differences in interpretation between what one party understood and what the other party wanted to say. However, excessive immersion in bureaucratic processes causes the main reason for that contract to be lost of sight, and doubts regarding a contractual detail may be used to defraud the expectations of the other. Often, the legal framework of the contract provides excuses for non-compliance. An effective judicial system needs to know how to avoid this. And Psychology shows that it is necessary that the inhibition of breach of contract be encouraged by society by considering twice the damage caused as the due compensation. With this move, society is finally able to feel that crime does not pay. The adoption of negative opportunistic behaviors will become unlikely because it will provoke a feeling of justice that Psychology today demonstrates to be the minimum limit for the human being to consider himself compensated for the loss that was imposed on him and the aggressor to feel that he was, precisely, diminished by the illegitimate gains that he sought to obtain.

One might think that negative opportunistic behavior acquires a space for action here. Easily, our mind will be plagued by the idea that some people will try to take advantage of others, claiming any breach of contract, just to obtain a gain. In this case, we will be facing a litigant in bad faith who, if proven, will also have to compensate for double the damages that he caused with his fraudulent action. Given our immense creativity, and given our bounded rationality, society cannot do without the presence of an effective judicial system. The advantages of a virtuous judicial system are not limited to the inhibition of negative opportunistic behaviors, but extend, above all, to the additional stimulation of positive opportunistic behaviors.

The "intelligent use of software" thus acquires decisive importance for society to checkmate negative opportunistic behavior. All of the above measures require a database that is solid, secure, and reliable. Information on which human decision-making can be grounded. People will be able to make their decisions based on facts, moved by their situational analysis, and free from prejudices and pressures of any kind. Instead of focusing on actions that will allow them to exploit others, each person will be aware of how important they are to the remaining members of society. The individual will be focused on doing well what he likes to do, on dedicating himself to professional activities that give him pleasure and will be aware of the real value that society attributes to him in the execution of these tasks. The "intelligent use of software" is an indispensable tool to boost positive opportunistic behavior, making each individual try to make their own decisions, provided with the relevant information to them. The "intelligent use of software" is the move that allows us to guarantee the superiority of positive opportunistic behaviors in the game.

The society of a country that decides to put into practice these six moves to combat negative opportunistic behavior will be more successful than the one that does not.

But human society is made up of over eight billion people, and no one can be left out. If we leave someone out, then society assumes that a part of itself is uninteresting, or despicable. It will be like getting a "draw for drowned" or getting a "perpetual check". And we can win the match. It is enough for us to pay attention to the positioning of our pieces.

If global society guarantees the free movement of people, goods, and capital, then resources will naturally go to places that provide the best living conditions for people. It is irrefutable that the positive effects of Pisistratus's rule in Athens extended to other peoples of the Aegean Sea. And his government, from the time it began until it ended, did not last twenty years. If Angola opens its borders to the Portuguese, Spanish, and French, then many European businessmen will rush to Angola in order to take advantage of its natural resources. At the same time, many Angolans will flock to Portugal, Spain, and France to learn in universities, learn in European companies, and enjoy the highest salaries in Europe. If the four countries adopt the seven rules, the four societies will raise the quality of life for everyone, without exception, and will achieve, very quickly, an enviable social equity compared to today's reality.

With the unanimous implementation of these rules, in addition to enthusiastically encouraging positive opportunistic behavior, global society also inhibits negative opportunistic behavior, which harms everyone. Influence peddling, bribes, deceptive practices, strikes, protests, and the use of violence to guarantee exclusive access to natural resources, all of them, quite simply, cease to make sense. The seven rules ensure that work is duly rewarded, both for the employer's effort and for the employee's commitment. But the seven rules also make the possession of material goods just a natural consequence of people's aptitude for the function. In other words, what will matter to society is how property is used, not who owns it. Global society will then be in a position to strive for peace and security for all its members. No one is left out. Nobody is interested in that. We will be in a position to checkmate negative opportunistic behaviors.

"Serendipity"

Checkmate negative opportunistic behaviors is something only governments can do. In 1995, the sociologist Mark Suchman, in his fabulous academic article on legitimacy management, with the title "Managing legitimacy: strategic and institutional approaches", warned that organizations, as is the case of the governments of each country, need to "make sense" before society to avoid being questioned. However, he cautioned that organizations also need to actually "have value" and be a safeguard against a lack of common sense. The verification of this interdependence between institutions and society implies that governments will not be able to checkmate negative opportunistic behaviors without society, previously, legitimizing them to do so.

The first time I read the word "serendipity" was in an academic article. I had never heard it before. I had never read it. I did not know its meaning.

I went to the Portuguese-English dictionary and the translation came simply "random". However, this translation made no sense when placed in the context of the scholarly article I was reading. So I looked up the meaning of "serendipity" in the English dictionary.

Finally, I realized that "serendipity" means a happy discovery, or being lucky enough to find something precious unexpectedly. To me, for simplicity, "serendipity" means "lucky chance."

A few years ago, a "lucky chance" occurred that led me to deeply question human nature. On her "Facebook" wall, a friend of mine shared a video of an athletics race in which only young people with Down Syndrome participated. It was a track race and six or seven athletes were running, more or less accelerated, in a short-distance race. At a certain point, a later athlete, perhaps the penultimate in the race, steps on the edge of the track and falls. Immediately, the nearest athlete stopped and helped him to his feet. A few seconds later, all athletes in the race stopped, went back, and helped each other. They came together to the finish line. They were all winners.

My quest for a deep understanding of the functioning of society, in general, and of the economy, in particular, forced me to conclude that nobody is self-sufficient. And we all have unique talents that we can help others with. Additionally, each step, each study, and each analysis, often highlighted my own shortcomings. I realized that an extraordinary orchestra is made up of musicians who play drums, violins, pianos, flutes, trombones, trumpets, clarinets, cymbals, and many other instruments, but in which each artist is only an expert on his instrument. And I do not know how to play any.

Typically, an orchestra has more than eighty musicians, and these musicians naturally accept and trust the help and coordination of a conductor. It does not matter who the conductor is. It does not matter who is at the piano. It does not matter who plays the saxophone. Each person is focused on doing their job as best they can. And I really like listening to them.

By combining these mundane thoughts with David Ricardo's conclusion regarding society's widespread interest in opening up economies, I once again questioned myself about what is the essence of human nature. What does it truly mean to be human? Adopt competitive behaviors, as the lions did in the African savannah, or adopt cooperative behaviors, as the athletes with Down Syndrome did?

Recent research demonstrates that it is true that human beings develop other senses when they lose one. Thus, blind person improves their abilities of hearing, smell, touch, and even improvements in the person's cognitive abilities occur after losing their sight. On the other hand, in addition to the five senses, human beings also exhibit a situation of neurodiversity in which each person's brain works differently. When some people see, hear, and feel the world differently, we may be looking at a person with autism. Often, these people have unique capabilities that the so-called normal human being cannot achieve. Perhaps the essence of being human lies in the excesses of each of these characteristics, which, in people with Down Syndrome, stands out for a much more developed sense of mutual help. But David Ricardo demonstrated that we all need everyone, and so-called normal people need the genius that autistic, blind, deaf, mute, or people with Down Syndrome can provide, and that can never be imitated by a machine.

When the challenge between Deep Blue and Kasparov took place, it was a fluke that dictated the victory of the computer. According to information from the documentary "The Man vs. The Machine," published by American television ESPN in 2014, the computer, in the evaluation of each move, would be programmed to avoid the possibility of entering into an automatic repetition process, in eternal circles. If this situation occurred, the machine was prepared to produce a valid move according to the rules of chess, regardless of its suitability for the game situation in question. It is said that, on move #44 of the game that dictated Deep Blue's victory, the machine produced an illogical move according to the programmers. It is said that Kasparov was surprised and therefore incorrectly interpreted that the machine was following a superior strategy that he himself was not understanding. Reportedly, Kasparov's confusion led the Grandmaster to make mistakes and ultimately lose the match.

I do not know if a lucky chance can lead humanity to win the game. But I know that to win, society has an inevitable need to consolidate an institutional environment where cooperation, respect, and harmony are cultivated.

Today, our global society contains an organization that is much more dedicated to the debate of ideas than to situational analysis. The debate on a given theme puts the opinions of each participant face to face. Usually, participants use their arguments to justify their alleged solutions, without questioning their counterparts, honestly and genuinely, about the reason for their differences of opinion. The debate tends to be seen as a competition of individual "truths." This reality results in a set of behavioral disagreements that prevent the parties from coming together for a joint analysis of the situation at hand.

But to be human is to be able to depend on each other. To be human is to be able to tell others that they can depend on us, while at the same time trusting that we can depend on others. And at that moment, each person masters their own destiny. Learning to do this consistently is something that has yet to be done. I hope that, for you, this reading may have been a "lucky chance."